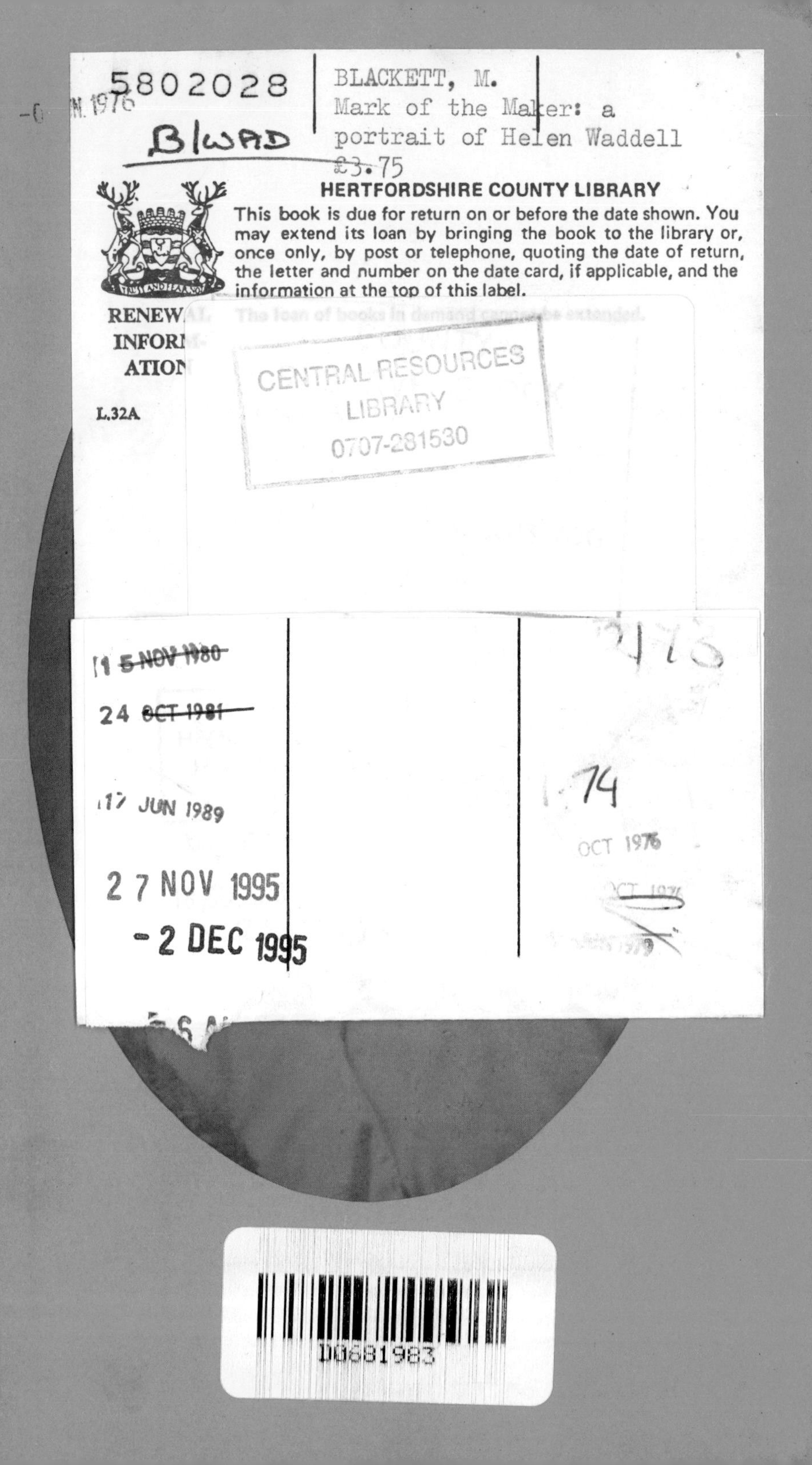

THE MARK OF THE MAKER

A Portrait of Helen Waddell

Helen Waddell at Columbia University, receiving an honorary degree, with (left to right) the Archbishop of St. Louis, President Butler of Columbia, and Mr Henry A. Wallace, Secretary of Agriculture. June 3 1935

THE MARK OF THE MAKER

A Portrait of Helen Waddell

MONICA BLACKETT

CONSTABLE
LONDON

First published in Great Britain 1973
by Constable & Company Ltd
10 Orange Street London WC2H 7EG

ISBN 0 09 459 100 8

Set in Monotype Perpetua
Printed in Great Britain
by Ebenezer Baylis and Son Limited
The Trinity Press, Worcester, and London

For Mollie and the family
at Kilmacrew

Contents

Introduction

This book is far from being a definitive biography, but it is an authentic portrait. It is the result of well over thirty years of deepening friendship between Helen Waddell and me, based on similar clerical parentage, a similar struggle against poverty to acquire education for a large family, as well as on our shared joys and sorrows from the moment we were introduced by my eldest brother.

Helen died in March 1965, and in August of that year I went to Kilmacrew in County Down to visit her sister, Margaret Martin, who was already a friend of mine. For hours we talked of Helen, and before I left, Meg had not only told me they had kept up a completely uninhibited correspondence from childhood, but also that she had collected every word from or about Helen on which she could lay hands. Then she showed me a huge Victorian chest of drawers, full to bursting with unsorted papers and undated letters, and she begged me read and select for publication the chaotic mass, as she was too old, too feeble in health and too sadly involved, to undertake the task. I demurred at first, but eventually gave way when she declared firmly that no one else should read the letters, and she would burn them if I did not agree.

It has taken me some years to keep my promise, but every word I wrote was approved by Meg until her death, and since then by her daughter, Mollie, to whom all the material now belongs.

Meg was six years older than Helen, and in 1906 she married the Reverend John Martin, a Presbyterian minister who inherited a house and farmland at Magherally in County Down. Kilmacrew House from then on became the home of Helen's heart, although until her stepmother's death in 1919 she was tied by her Puritan sense of duty to taking care of the ageing invalid in a 'small, thin house with no garden' in Belfast.

Helen's own mother had died when she was only two years old, and as she was the youngest of ten children (eight boys and two girls), perhaps death was the only solution to the problem of being a Presbyterian missionary's wife. However, the bearded father loved his brood of children and soon selected a new Irish partner from his flock to look after them. Helen describes her father as a 'pioneer missionary in Manchuria and later in Japan, a sinologue and a saint; the Vicar of Wakefield turned Chinese scholar – a happy scholar too, for his magnum opus was to be *The Importance of the Trinity to the Chinese Mind*'. He died when Helen was eleven years old, soon after bringing his family home from Tokyo to go to school in Ulster.

Helen was not photogenic, perhaps because she had little claim to classic beauty of face or figure, perhaps because her supremely musical voice and the gentle articulateness of every word she spoke, made looks unimportant, even scarcely observed. Among the professional efforts to depict her, it is significant that only Grace Henry's portrait – a back view of her writing *The Desert Fathers* – catches her personality, whereas in real life it was almost tangible, radiating vitality and compassion.*

As Helen rarely assembled her papers, never numbered them, and scarcely ever dated her letters, editing them has taken several years. Selection has at times seemed an insoluble problem, and inevitably the originals (most of them handwritten) of her books, poems, lectures and miscellaneous writings, published or unpublished await further research.

I can only offer sincerest, grateful thanks to all her many friends and relations who contributed information and extra material: above all to Meg, the sister who preserved every word or mention of Helen she could. Regrettably there are no letters from Meg to Helen.

*The front view of her with three distinguished Americans at a Conferring of Degrees at Columbia University in New York which is reproduced as the frontispiece is a perfect characteristic likeness.

To Mollie Martin, Meg's only daughter and Helen's much-loved niece, I am deeply indebted for endorsing her mother's request to make use of the material, and for her consistent co-operation and assistance throughout the years.

Many thanks are also due to Helen's literary executor, Mr Harold Rubinstein, and to all those from whom I have received information and/or permission to quote. It is a long list: no one refused, in fact most expressed their enthusiasm for Helen and her works: Lord Baldwin of Bewdley, Lord David Cecil, Lord Clark, Lady Ogilvie, Mr John Sparrow, Mrs Michael Sadleir, Mrs Barbara Vere-Hodge, Dr Mayne Waddell, Mme de Praingy (née Nicole Vaudremer), Mr George Buchanan, Mr Feliks Topolski, Miss Helen Alford, Mrs Gladys Bendit, Miss Marjorie Broughall, Miss Naomi Mitchison, Miss Eiluned Lewis, Mrs Doreen Smithells, Miss Constance Babington-Smith, on behalf of Miss Rose Macaulay, W. M. Heinemann Ltd, administrator of the Beerbohm Estate on behalf of Max Beerbohm, A. M. Heath & Co. on behalf of Mr Diarmid Russell for 'AE' – his late father, and Mr Peter Davies. I have also to thank Sir Rupert Hart-Davis for his advice on punctuation, and to express my gratitude and pleasure at being published by Constable, the firm that played so vital a part in Helen's life and left me with so many compulsive memories. Finally, I wish to thank my own daughter, Honor Sharman, not only for producing legible typescripts, but also for comments and suggestions from a younger generation.

This book has been a labour of love to write: I can only end the Introduction as I began: it is a portrait, not a definitive biography.

Monica Blackett 1973

CHAPTER I

Childhood and Education

No account of Helen's life could be written without personal knowledge of her sister's family and the house at Kilmacrew, Co. Down, for to her they were a constant magnetic point, amounting to an obsession in later years.

Meg's husband owned Kilmacrew House (usually called 'Killy') and about 120 acres of mixed agricultural land, which included woodland, a peat bog called 'the Moss', and a narrow but fast-flowing river that habitually forced an impetuous flood whenever rain fell more heavily than usual. An avenue of trees of all ages and sizes, oak and ash, lime and chestnut, elm and beech, interspersed with fir, curves for two hundred yards from the road to the early eighteenth-century farmhouse in its deep hollow. The long low house is built of stone; its solid walls are creeper-covered, and its windows are set deep into their stone surrounds. The roof is stone-tiled and luxuriant with lichen. Behind the house is the farmyard with stables, cowsheds and the modern but quaintly shaped silo: some walls are whitewashed and the roofs of all the buildings are steeply sloped and moss-covered. It is an artist's dream but a functional nightmare. In the garden, flowers, vegetables and weeds grow in amazing profusion and to a great size. An orchard of ancient fruit-trees lies along one side of the house; and a spectacular pear-tree, its trunk and every branch blanketed with moss, darkens some of the windows, but is so luminescent with white blossom in spring that no one has ever had the heart to cut back a twig of it.

This is the house and land that figure so large in Helen's letters. Its spell is undeniable and almost tactual, but not in the least sinister. Somehow, over it lies beauty, and the glory behind or beyond tragedy, that Helen instinctively searched for and wrote about all her life.

'J.D.' and Meg had five children, a daughter Mary (always known as Mollie), and four sons, Sydney, Jack, Charlie and George, in that order. Helen shared them all with their parents: they were part of her life. To Meg she once wrote: 'I think we two are rather like a tree that forked so near the root it looks like two trees: but in the earth there's only one.' She used her small nephews and niece as an audience for testing a series of biblical stories for children that she contributed to a Presbyterian magazine every week.

Helen spoke often of her 'enchanted childhood in Japan', and made use of it in the legends and fairy tales that are among her earliest writings. Very soon after the family's return to Ulster, her father and stepmother took Meg and Helen to be interviewed by Mrs Byers (later Lady Byers), foundress of The Victoria School for Girls in Belfast, and at this period, still its first headmistress. After accepting both girls, Mrs Byers cast a piercing eye on Helen and said: 'This one I will educate for nothing.' Her perception received a high reward, for during the seven years of schooling Helen won enough prizes and scholarships to make her a profitable investment for any headmistress.

A letter from Helen to her sister after her last year and final examinations paints the picture of her schooldays.

> I wanted to tell you all about my exams myself. . . . Every day for a week I rushed into Uncle John's digs to look at the paper, but I vowed on Saturday that I wouldn't cross the doorstep again, I was so cross. Then at 2 o'clock, posty brings a letter of congratulation from Mrs Byers for my brilliant successes. Thinks I, 'I've got the class prize all round', and I rushed in for the paper.
>
> Alas, my love, I have but one first prize – though it's more than I thought I would get – and that's in English. And the prize I thought I was sure of nearly – French – went to Mary Darragh. However, I'm only one and a half marks behind her, and I'm doing my best to forgive her. Also I am second in Latin, and

what I am proudest of, a third prize in Maths! Dear, I feel it is a pity to go on with one's career; is it not better to retire gracefully at a moment like this? ME, a prize in pure mathematics! . . . I was looking up the marks in Wylie's office, and to my woe saw that if there hadn't been a second paper I'd have been first in both Maths and Latin! I got 81 on the morning paper in Latin, but I knew myself that I'd done badly on the evening. But I could love Gregory* for the English paper he gave me 84 and wrote a note on the prize lists that 'Miss Waddell's paper was exceptionally good'!!! So there are compensations. The four prizes come to £2 19s. 9d. I do think they might have spared the threepence and made it £3! Alas, it all goes on books – all but 14s. 9d. which is ordered on Strains for binding. As if I want their dirty old calf on my nice clean books! I'd rather have it in a new pair of boots. . . . As for the First Arts exams, they might have been worse. I didn't like the Latin paper awfully – they gave a long string of fragments of lines, and asked you to annotate the same. Which is sheer cruelty.

You never can tell how you've done on a French paper. But the English! The morning man was a Reverend Professor, and he asked us to discuss Milton's claims to greatness, also Wordsworth's, also their differences, and to sketch the English prose style, and to discuss the 'romantic' elements of Keats and Byron. Luckily I remembered quotations, and I went on my way rejoicing. And the precious old dear set a comp. on the 'greatness of Shakespearean Drama'. I hope I did not make him ill. I tried to restrain myself, and I racked my brains for inspiration – but nothing would come except 'England owes much to the severity of a country squire', and I felt I had grown beyond that. Gregory set the evening paper, and as it was mostly on 'Julius Caesar' and very little on the books, I wrote him four books with great internal satisfaction.

But dear knows, I paid up the next day. I was written out. I think you can guess what I was like when I nearly went mad over the little preliminary to a question 'What are poles and

*Gregory Smith, Professor of English.

polars?' But really, Meg, there's more in that than meets the eye, and if I hadn't taken drastic measures I'd be there yet! But I think I got two perfectly right on the morning paper – Trig, Calculus and Geometry, and some that may be. And I did better in the evening. The Physics papers were queer; and I don't know if they're good or bad. But really by the time Saturday came we were past caring! Darragh and I were the only two who took the Blue papers right through, and the superintendent looked respectful when it came to Saturday. But every afternoon a barrel organ came round and played 'Antonio'. Get Geo* to whistle it to you, and you'll guess what you feel like. . . . Give my respectful salutations to Geo and tell him I am living to see him in his dog collar.

In 1908 Helen, at the age of nineteen, began her first year at Queen's College, Belfast. She read Latin, English, French, Mathematics and Experimental Physics, and in her second and third years English Language and Literature. The scholar in her blossomed: she won more prizes and scholarships, and three at least of the professors whose lectures she attended recognised genius in her work. Between Alfred Dixon and Gregory Smith a rivalry arose when the former tried to entice the brilliant pupil away from literature to mathematics. But neither of them had the attraction for Helen that the bearded face and flattering attention of the famous Visiting Professor in English had. George Saintsbury came from Edinburgh and his renown was at its height: he examined Helen and marvelled, and he remained her 'literary god'. They met seldom but corresponded frequently until his death. He, and to a lesser extent Gregory Smith, had the greatest influence on her imagination, on her mind and her intelligence.

There was, however, another side to Helen – a pleasure-loving one. She entered into all the student activities at Queen's that had her stepmother's approval. The frustrations of the care of a narrow-minded invalid were a grievous burden about which she wrote in letters to Meg and also in a few lines of verse:

*Helen's youngest brother George.

I stood within the empty House of Youth,
Hearing a far-off footfall on the road,
And hearing waited, knowing for a truth
They were the feet of life that nearer trod.

It seemed to me the very emptiness
Crept close to me and fell a-listening too:
I held my breath for very blessedness,
And still the sound of footsteps nearer drew.

I did not know that they had come so near.
No faltering I heard, nor any stay,
Until it struck upon me, listening there,
The accent of a step that goes away.

In 1910, while still at Queen's, she tells Meg:

Don't be vexed with me for not having answered at once – dear knows your letter would have drawn a reply from Buddha himself, but that paper for the Christian Union was promised for Friday and I only got a week's notice. And I have done nothing but eat and drink and sleep the Non-Christian Religions since last Saturday. Do you wonder, Meg, I feel half dead? They wanted a half-hour's paper and they got it. And they wanted me to write on the 'Challenge of the Religions' and they got it. This is what I took as the challenge – 'We had a great creed and we have outgrown it; you had a great creed and you have outgrown it'. It was an awful paper to write. But you can guess the effect of same when Billy Lynd told me the day before that he would refuse to chairman my paper because he would bust with suppressed giggles: and the same Billy Lynd, after I had sat down, got to his feet and peremptorily closed the meeting with the benediction before anybody could say anything. The notices were 'Discussion Invited', and when this was pointed out to him afterwards, he retorted savagely: 'It would do them more good to go home and think about it. I wasn't going to spoil the thing with their prating.'

Then I came home in an awful depression. I suppose it is the reaction. But I know that every bone in me is crying out for you – and the babies. I want to get away from C.U.s and Bible Circles and Classes, and the notices of dances to which I am not going, and the occasional glimpses of people that I want to fool with and never get the chance. And I want to smell the old fields and chop onions for you at dinner, and shudder at Sydney's step on the stair, and him on top of me. 'Lay this earth upon thy heart, and thy sickness shall depart.' Meg, I'm specially bad because this is Dudley week, and Queen's is going mad. The teams from Cork and Galway arrive on Monday: match played that afternoon. Reception at 7, dance on Wednesday at 7. Do you wonder, my love, that the World and the Flesh seem very lusty inside me this weather?

Mother took two sittings last Sunday for we had heard Moody twice and liked him better each time. He seems awfully decent, has a big good-natured face and preaches really splendidly. And you certainly feel better when you're paying your way. And Mr and Mrs Moody are coming for tea tomorrow, so the house will be putting its best foot forward.

By 1911 Helen had realised her future was in creative writing.

Peggy, Peggy, my wits are somewhere I am not. . . . I do not want to do research. I do not want to write anything for ever and ever Amen. I want to eat gooseberries and talk in our unintellectual manner to Sydney and Jack. You made my mouth water. The one thing I am thankful for at this minute is that I haven't got to choose my subject for the studentship till October. Gregory warned me that my subject would need to be good to pass the Faculty in October – 'for it will stand some criticism. You see, this is the first time the Studentship has ever been awarded'. And I am to get that Jap thing typed, and if possible write one or two things more. I have written another, by name 'White Iris', which beats the first one hollow, but it's maybe on the principle of the new baby. But Gregory is on his holidays now, and I'll wait till September.

And I gave him that legend – 'Quia non sanctus erat', and I think he was more taken with it than anything I've done for him. 'I particularly like your motif.' And I am to elaborate it with a 10th-century background.

Next year's work will be queer. I'm not to be allowed to do 'an imaginative piece of belles lettres like your Marius'. It's to be an edition of an unpublished MS – or something equally appalling. He wanted me to go to London and the British Museum. But I set my foot down on that.

Darling, I had an enthusiastic letter of congrats from Cousin Harry: 'In you the Waddell intellect hath flowered and reached its apogee'!!

CHAPTER II

Dr Taylor and Professor Saintsbury

Helen had other friends outside the university besides the professors, but they, too, tended to have flowing beards and to be of her stepmother's generation and, of course, strictly Presbyterian. Helen's favourite was the Reverend George Taylor. It is possible he had known her father before the turn of the century, which would have made the appeal of his still-handsome, bearded face almost irresistible to her.

In 1914, the dedicated Presbyterian missionary and his wife spent a well-earned furlough in Belfast from their work in India. They met Helen in her stepmother's house: their friendship was sealed immediately. Adoption in spirit followed from that day and the father-daughter relationship was soon established, as shown by the weekly letters to and from India until his death in 1920. He and his wife were childless; both loved Helen and the record is one of comfort and joy to all concerned. It is also a source of information about Helen's development in her 'lost decade'.

Inevitably the main subject in their exchange of letters had, especially at first, a strong flavour of religion, but Helen's articulate honesty soon widened this to whatever was uppermost in her mind at the time of writing, and the letters from her new 'father' lose the didactic touch and become as simple and responsive as a brother's. Indeed the alteration in tone seems to have been brought about by the instantaneous death in 1915 of her youngest brother George, through an entirely unexpected heart attack. (He was a Presbyterian minister in a parish near Kilmacrew and Helen often helped him with his sermons.) She wrote long letters to Dr Taylor about the sudden tragedy and its effect on her.

> I remember one letter that came from you that Monday after his burying. You spoke of your fear that I should marry for protection and not for love. It is quite possible that I shall not marry at all. I did not like any of the few people who have wanted me. It's not that I am difficult, for I've known at least two men I would probably have fallen in love with if they hadn't been married already. (I'm not laughing). Just that they were the type that contented me.

If Dr Taylor had lived long enough to read Helen's novel *Peter Abelard*, he might not have misunderstood: she longed far more to protect than to be protected, but first she had to admire and respect and then to glorify and worship.

Certainly Dr Taylor approved more highly of her scriptural studies and the tales she told her Sunday School class, than of her interest in medieval authors, religious and secular, including Rabelais. Here she defends herself:

> I've been thinking that the problem of what is and is not for the glory of God, is more or less solved by Christ's 'Take heed to your spirit'. I have a horror of 'novels with a purpose'. And I think most genuine things are grown on the principle of 'Consider the lilies of the field'. I was thinking of the lilies of the field when I said that most of the things in the world exist only because they are beautiful. Why may not I write pretty things that come into my head when God Himself spent most of His creative faculty in making things good to look at? I was working at the English Renaissance in my thesis the other day, and struck out this – I do not know whether it is true or not – that the difference between the thought of the Middle Ages and the thought of the Elizabethan Renaissance is largely this, that the medieval conception of right and wrong widens into the Renaissance conception of good and evil. 'Good that is pleasantness and beauty as well as sound morality, evil that is suffering and ugliness and sin.'
>
> It hurts me when people beg me to write with a purpose. Not you – but some other people, rather narrow people. . . .

I asked them in desperation one day if it was justifiable for them to spend their time making a specially nice-looking pudding, when I was criminal for having spent a morning over a string of verses that had absolutely no 'moral' value – but just that they sang themselves with a nice wee chime. It's as necessary to have nice things to put in your head as nice things to put in your 'society' as Mr Witherow would say.

I spoke of those Chinese Lyrics of mine, and asked you how they struck you – from the straiter standpoint? But you do not tell me.

Listen, one allows an artist to draw things because they are beautiful. You don't ask him to point a moral – or to deal only with things symbolic or sacred. I know I have seen more of the 'peace of God' in a wee sketch of a folding of the hills, than in any picture of the Good Shepherd.

Don't you think after all it comes to this – that a good tree brings forth good fruit? And that you've got to 'take heed to your spirit'?

It's extraordinary how things straighten out when you get one of those rare glimpses of the Person of Christ. Someone quoted to me reprovingly the other day à propos of this blessed useless research work of mine:

'Take my lips and let me sing
Always, only for my King.'

– a hymn that always leaves me unhappy and artificial and strained. (By the way, the great inspirations have come to me more often from people who can write secular as well as sacred verse – secular is a pagan word. 'What God hath cleansed, call not those. . . .') And I was my most rebellious.

And all at once as I ramped at the narrowness and bigotry of people, it seemed to me I had a glimpse of Him going down a sunny road. And I collapsed, not so much into penitence for my railing, but into sudden comprehension. 'The Son of Man came eating and drinking', and yet. . . .

I *must* stop, and I have said nothing I meant, and said it so badly. Don't try to make it coherent. Just go on liking me, for it's personality – His above all – that saves us.

Your
HELEN

Helen met Professor Saintsbury socially for the first time at a dinner-party given by Professor Gregory Smith in 1914. It was a great occasion for her. In a letter to Dr Taylor thanking him for a cheque he sent her, she tells him she is spending part of it on 'that white satin evening dress of mine veiled in primrose chiffon. It's two years old, and will have to be a little different – for Saintsbury's dinner. And I have never worn primrose in my life, and I've always hankered after it. I have a passion for yellow.'

No letters exist describing either Helen's or Professor Saintsbury's reactions to the dinner-party, but its importance is amply recorded by the lively correspondence to which it gave birth. Young men sometimes accused Helen of lack of 'fundamental reality', not realising that her refuge from responsibility might lie in fantasy. She could write to Dr Taylor without insincerity or inhibition as 'Father', and to Saintsbury as 'Your Excellency' or 'My Lord', and the older men understood and accepted. (Later Helen writes of these and similar expressions as 'a game we played'.) She does, however, tell Meg about Saintsbury's visit to her home soon after the party:

Och dear, sure the Professor has turned up again – yesterday evening to be accurate. Top hat and frock coat and all. If he had any idea how my very soul revolts at them he'd give them to an 'old clothes'. We had other visitors, but he manfully sat on, and when they took their leave he came and knelt on the carpet where I was industriously packing away the infant's china teaset, and handed me the things, and looked upon me with wistful beamy spectacles. And he told me he was growing homesick for the Paris boulevards – the uplift of heart and gaiety of it. 'Sort of "I care for nobody and nobody cares for me" feeling?' says I innocently. The Professor looked reproachful. 'No,' he said, 'that's not the attraction. . . . In fact, that is what hurts. I swore when I left Paris the last time that I would never come back alone.'

I digressed on Gregory Smith's weakness for a fortnight in London at the theatres! And I was beginning to tell him about my job this year – that Gregory had said I was too young to begin to write, when he interrupted at the 'too young'. 'I think I'd agree with him,' he said heavily. 'You are – too young. I wish you were – older.' Meg, is he going to keep doing sentry-go between this and Edinburgh till I've sense to eat what's set before me?

As is only natural, religion colours Helen's earliest excursions into print, both in poetry and prose. No doubt her stepmother understood the latter best, but her encouragement hardly extended to novels, and plays were of the devil. Her special approval was reserved for the versions of Bible stories which Helen wrote for her Sunday School class and which were printed in *Daybreak*, a weekly Presbyterian magazine.

Few of her early poems reveal her latent power over words, but before her stepmother died, she felt free to spread her wings, and the theme of love, sacred and profane, absorbed her completely. The intensity of her capacity to lose herself in the emotions of others, and by understanding to reproduce them, added to her scholarly facility for languages, notably medieval Latin and French, which was often as startling to herself as to her professors. All her life she remained drawn to creative, direct or indirect, translation.

If publication is a criterion of success, then Helen's début into the world of literature can be fixed in 1915, the year Constable & Co. brought out the first edition of *Lyrics from the Chinese*. Four years earlier Helen had written to Meg:

Do you remember the old shelf of 'Chinese Classics' by James Legge, D.D., Trubner and Co., London and Hong Kong? The very name of it is an incantation. I've worked beside it for years and dipped into most of them, dull dogs enough, chiefly sayings of emperors and sages. Well, it happened on Tuesday. I had sickened my soul over Jean de Meung* and yearned for anything by way of dry disinfectant. And I reached out to the familiar shelf, and something guided my hand to one of the volumes I had never opened before. It opened itself at: 'The gourd has still its bitter leaves', and I found that I was reading the prose translations of odes that were 'sung at the court of Soo in the 29th year of the Duke Seang', in the sixth century before Christ.

Darling, my breath came thick, my head swam round, for I know buried treasure when I see it, and not even the Reverend James Legge's awful and literal prose could hide the freshness of it. And in ten minutes I had written this. I'm going to give you the prose first. (By the way it's the cry of a woman who has turned her back on marriage for the sake of love.)

> The gourd has still its bitter leaves,
> And the crossing at the ford is deep.
> If deep, I will go through with my clothes on,
> If shallow, I will do so holding them up.
>
> The ford is full to overflowing,
> There is the note of the female pheasant.
> The full ford will not wet the axle of my carriage,
> It is the pheasant calling for her mate.
>
> The boatman keeps beckoning,
> And others cross with him, but I do not,
> I am waiting for my friend.

I do not think you'll be disappointed at my lyrical rendering of it:

> The gourd has still its bitter leaves,
> And deep the crossing at the ford.
> I wait my lord.

*The thirteenth-century French poet who continued the *Roman De La Rose*, and translated the letters of Abelard and Héloise into French.

The ford is brimming to its banks;
The pheasant cries upon her mate,
My lord is late.

The boatman still keeps beckoning,
And others reach their journey's end.
I wait my friend.

I did about half a dozen more and sent them to Gregory last night. He saw me in the library today, and came straight for me. I was expecting a 'I think you had better finish your serious work first, and then you might do something with them'. As a matter of fact, my 'serious work' is apparently thrown to the winds. 'Have you any more?' was his first demand. 'Here, come into my room for a minute.' So I went. He was rushing to his lecture, but he was for once roused. 'Go on with them? Certainly, by all means, and bring them to me.'

Helen reports intermittently to Meg after this and her moods vary:

Well dear, I have seen Gregory again. And I am to work on the lyrics until I have enough to fill a book, get them typed, 'and then I'll help you to hawk them round', says Gregory with his slow smile. 'And I may drop the pre-Shakespearean woman just for a little?' says I eagerly. Gregory remembers that he is Professor of English Literature: 'I was just thinking when I got your MSS this morning that she was rather in the background. And (his gravity is portentous) if these lyrics of yours hadn't been so exceptional, I am afraid you would have heard from me today.' Meg, that man is a joy to me.

You'll get a collected letter some time soon, after my next meeting with Gregory. The first seven lyrics have swelled to twenty-three. None of them is as good as my first, but I don't think I'll ever do anything as good in my life again. You were such a duck to say what you did. If you had not liked them, do you know even Gregory's praise would have fallen flat. He went through every one of the twenty, criticising and appraising. But my triumph was when he came to one that I had hesitated about sending him. It was too elaborate a thought for the old simplicity. But I knew it was a musical thing, so I sent it – how musical I didn't know till he began reading it aloud. Peggy, he believes I'll do something yet. He said something about 'a young woman of my ambition' and I said, 'I'm not a particularly ambitious person'. 'You have reason to be,' says Gregory very quietly, 'but I'm not going to tell you what I think of your powers.'

For the next three years the *Chinese Lyrics* fell so much into the background that no mention of them exists. Perhaps Helen was too absorbed in other work. Queen's University gave her the degree of B.A., with First Class Honours in English, in 1911; M.A. in 1912 – for which Professor Saintsbury examined her. The subject of her thesis was 'Milton, the Epicurist'. Perhaps more frequent meetings occurred between the sisters. Dr Taylor was uninterested in secular poetry, so Helen would not have discussed the lyrics with him. However, by June 1915 all was well and Helen was writing excitedly to Meg:

I heard from Constable this morning. I had written to ask them to send me another half dozen and incidentally inquired if they were selling still. They answer in their most businesslike and unimpressive manner that they have sold – nine hundred and four! Peggy, if you only knew the grey despair of some days when I couldn't write, and when there were no reviews! But the reaction is so strong it has turned me half dizzy. I am still a little breathless – 904 . . . 904! And at best I hoped for 450 or 500. IT'S SUCCESS.

After this, Wednesday's excitement falls flat, though I was greatly lifted at the time. Constable wrote briefly that they had received an application for permission to set some of the Lyrics to music. Would I agree? I was enchanted. For if the songs were popular, it would be the best possible advertisement. Gregory is his very nicest about it, and wants me to send one to Professor Saintsbury . . . and bless you, the Lyrics will do yet.

This morning there came a letter from Brussels, from the Society of 'Études Sino-Belges' to ask would I present them with a copy of my book for review in the journal 'Chine et Belgique' which is widely circulated both in China and in Europe.

And Mother met Sam* in town this afternoon, and he nearly did a *pas seul* in Donegal Place when he heard of the nine hundred. And he says they are talking greatly of the Lyrics in Dublin, and George Russell (AE) did me an article in the 'Irish Homestead' two months ago which I never saw.

Helen's decision to stay in Belfast and nurse her stepmother shows courage and determination. It was not taken lightly or blindly. Even in 1912 she tells Meg: '. . . things began happening on Friday week. Gregory telephoned me to come for an interview at 12. It was Oxford all over again. And he laid himself out to say whatever he could, and it was a good deal. He quoted Saintsbury to me. He said that he himself had never met a student as clever as your humble (anything but humble) servant, whether man or woman: that if my literary career were to close now, it would be a loss not only to myself, but to "your subject and, in fact, to the world".'

A letter to Dr Taylor written retrospectively in 1916 is relevant:

I want to tell you – and I think it will please you more than anything – that you have somehow helped 'to justify the ways of God' in fact. For once or twice I have wondered of late, notably under influenza, if I were right in giving up Oxford for what Gregory thought an unnecessary scruple. It's about four years ago since he urged me to it, and I took it then for 'the kingdoms of the world and the glory of them'. It didn't seem possible to vex my mother and leave her alone. . . . He

*Helen's eldest brother, actor and playwright in Dublin.

warned me that I had ruined myself as far as academic high places went; that it probably meant my life was to be literary and not academic. He twinkled in spite of himself – perhaps on the whole I would have a better time.

I have a curious feeling that I have come to the end of something. What helps to emphasise the end of the chapter is that there's every prospect of Gregory Smith's departure. Saintsbury has resigned, and the papers are fairly unanimous in naming Gregory as his successor. I shall miss him more than I like to think, for he was my literary Father Confessor. And I think we both of us enjoyed the relationship.

He was so perverse and indolent and kindly, and his criticism was of an extraordinary 'fine-ness'. He hadn't Saintsbury's breadth nor his humanity, but he had more subtlety – and I have to admit an extraordinary baffling charm. He was one of the best-hated men in Queen's – and he knew it.

I'll maybe write to you about the Rabelais matter when I'm more in the academic humour. But dear, don't be too hard on Rabelais. Remember that I have read enormously in fifteenth-century literature, and it is very foulspoken. And yet I think I would be 'outraged' as easily by language as I was at fifteen. And you know, I think Rabelais was one of the great henchmen of the New Faith. And he was – I'm certain of it – religious: in the fullest meaning of the word.

Saintsbury's resignation did not hit Helen so hard: their friendship had always been kept alive by letters. Saintsbury encouraged her and actively helped her career. The contrast between her attitude to him and to Dr Taylor is vividly brought out when Saintsbury in 1916 published a book of essays: one was on Rabelais and he sent the proofs to Helen:

Excellency, kind Excellency,

Say that you did not send the last sheet of the Rabelais proofs and put me out of my misery. For I can find it nowhere. . . . Excellency, you know that I am wretched about it. Will it matter dreadfully? I am hoping against hope that

> you overlooked it. It has left me without heart to talk to you about the rest of it.
>
> You know I am never intelligent about the organisation of a book – other people may praise you for your fieldmarshalling. It's your suggestive quality I like. There were many phrases I meant to commend – one especially on the 'sheep-like habit of the Middle Ages'. And in the Rabelais part I liked especially the paragraph where you 'got' Panurge. I did not think it was possible. And again your noting that cruel paragraph on Pierocole. It hurts more than anything in Rabelais. But nothing in your proofs is anything but vanity beside the chapter on the *Matter of Britain*. Will you forgive this impertinence? That I never dreamt with a style so turbulent and of so distinctive a 'headmark' as yours, you could translate as you do. Is it any use to entreat you to do more of the Vulgate – a book of it? But it is mercy I should be asking, not graces.
>
> I am too remorseful about that Rabelais proof to be happy with you. I know you will not be *very* angry: but you can't help being irritated.

In her Belfast days Helen wrote delightful fairy tales and legends based on Japanese, Chinese, Indian and Persian, as well as European sources. Some of these stories are of biographical interest relating to her childhood in Japan. In 1917 she tells Professor Saintsbury:

> I'm doing a new lot of fairy tales for Arnold & Co. – French, Italian and Spanish. None of the series is to be published until the price of paper goes down. I was sorry; I wanted you to have *The Princess Splendour*. I've just finished *Puss in Boots*; such a nice formal Puss, in the manner of the eighteenth century. One feels that that manner comes naturally to cats. But one word baffles me; I can't equal Perrault's* last sentence – 'Le chat devint grand seigneur'.

*Charles Perrault (*d.* 1705), French poet and critic.

Helen also wrote a play, *The Spoilt Buddha*, which was staged in Belfast, with her brother Sam Waddell in the chief part. She had asked Saintsbury to read the MS. He replied:

> I shall be delighted to read the play (that is 'foi de Saintsbury' again) and no nonsense. I am not a theatre-goer, but some inveterate playhouse-haunters have told me that I know a good play when I see it, even off the stage. *Now I* shall read the thing in cool blood and tell you what I think of it. I really believe that as a critic I *can't* lie. 'You find it easy, Sir, in other relations?' you say, gathering the purple amice round your virgin form. I do not choose to continue the conversation on that head or in that style. I only know that I am very sorry you should have been dissatisfied or distressed in any way. For you know you have the mark of the Maker on your forehead. 'Be grateful for this, young woman.'
>
> Which I am yours and I hope
> His truly,
> G.S.

During this same 'lost decade' Helen had tried her hand at journalism, but she soon realised it was not her line. Writing to Dr Taylor she says: 'The Editor of the *Standard* wrote to me last week asking for a 1,500 word article, if possible with an undercurrent of the war. I am depressed: I doubt I'll ever be a journalist, for writing to order is beyond me.' But her articles and reviews were, even during the First World War, accepted by the *Manchester Guardian*, *The Nation*, *Blackwood's* and other magazines.

Correspondence with Dr Taylor was brought to an end by his death at the beginning of 1920. Helen spoke of him all her life with admiration and great affection. Years later in 1935, writing retrospectively to Meg, she says:

> You know, the one thing I learned out of those last years in Cedar Avenue, was that to hate is to be in hell. I didn't actually hate Mother; but I had a deep festering grudge against all the

ways she had thwarted me, the things she had taken from me, and never a word of thanks: all the sacrifices were on her side. After she was dead, I suddenly saw my own heart. And I knew that if only I had mastered that grudge inwardly as well as outwardly, those years would have been far richer. I suppose death helps to put things under the countenance of eternity. It wasn't that I was sorrier for her after she died – it was partly my pity for her that used to drive me so crazy: a mixture of anger and pity comes near murder. It was that I had let a grievance poison myself. And a grievance is a kind of cancer of the heart.

Darling, I have so marvelled at you all these years, not only your courage, but your soundness and sweetness. Don't let the dark tide that is in us all of bitterness against men and God come any higher. Generosity is far more important than any chastity; and don't constrict God's infinity of kindness by making bargains with him.

The 'lost decade' was over, but neither Helen nor Meg were ever embittered: the strength of gentleness was theirs.

CHAPTER III

Oxford

In February 1919, Helen's stepmother died suddenly. She tells Saintsbury in a note from Kilmacrew House:

> It's wet, and the candle is blowing at the open window and there is a corncrake out in the dark. And I have felt human again for the first time. My mother died last Friday in her sleep. I found her, in the chair.
>
> I suppose it is the reaction after the long years. But I came down here dead. Not that I was grieving – except that bitter remorse for all the unkind things you ever did or said. Just I didn't care what became of me. I was free at last – and there was nothing on earth that I wanted to do.
>
> I don't much yet. But this is an old house and they're all young, and they like me awfully. And Peggy and I wandered the lanes for hours, and it was raining a little, and you know the smell of wet honeysuckle.

And two months later when she was leaving the Belfast house she says:

> I'm sitting on the last chair before the vanmen take it from me; the only cheerful thing in the house is the fire. And, in a fashion, myself.
>
> For I was not happy in this house, Excellency, except that I wrote to you from it. And also there is something in St James': 'Behold, we count them happy which endure.'
>
> And now I've got almost every one of the things I beat

against the bars for. And I am so happy that, being a Northerner, I am afraid.

But now as then,
Your
HELEN

The very next year Helen's friend, Dr Taylor, died suddenly in India. Shortly before his death she had written to thank him for his gift of books and money and tell him about her birthday:

It was a nice birthday. There was a note from Saintsbury by the midday post, with an exquisite Brussels lace handkerchief – 'peradventure to make it more precious you will carry it on your wedding-day' – and with a scrap of pastiche, as he calls it:

'A ta trentième,
O ma Lointaine
Princesse.
Moi, je t'adore
Bien plus encore,
Sans cesse.'

And all the day was May at its loveliest. All Friday I lay in a wood above the Lough, deep in wild hyacinths, and watched the haze make Cave Hill like the 'great vision of the guarded mount'. . . . I am wondering if the Toad story has not reached you – *The Doorkeeper of Buddha*? Tell me and I'll send another.

Helen was thirty years old when she became the arbiter of her own destiny. In November 1920 she arrived in Oxford to fulfil the conditions of residence for the Ph.D. of that University, and to begin a study of the secular origins of the stage, which finally resolved itself into a book on *The Wandering Scholars*.

Her decision to choose Somerville College was greatly influenced by the fact that her Belfast friend, Maude Clark, was a history don there. England and Oxford were almost foreign countries to her and she never felt truly at home in either. Her temperament was basically Irish, not Anglo-Saxon or monarchical. Her sense of history saved her, though it was medieval Europe which caught her sympathetic perception most vividly of all.

Not only had the gulf of years to be faced as she returned to university life, but she had first to recognise that her own awareness, intellectual and emotional, had developed as it were in the dark. She accepted the loneliness of freedom quickly, and dramatised herself and her surroundings to Meg in her first letters; but after altering all the furniture she got used to her attic in Keble Road as well as to her immersion in overwhelming female company.

'Oxford itself is lovely,' she wrote, 'and the only way is to see it alone.' And a week or so later: 'Oxford is growing on me very slowly.' In a short month her tone changes:

> Oxford is full of bells, some of them jangling, but now and then Big Tom speaks: he puts you in a good humour in spite of yourself . . . I've still to see the gardens. It's a generous place. 'John's' garden is open to anyone, and it is said to be the loveliest in Oxford, but no place is private. You're as free as in a cathedral. Curious, I like it best when I am alone in it. Its sense of the past came to me in the Bodleian. I'm getting into the way of working there, but it's painful. Like disused machinery. The bit I'm doing just now – Latin liturgical play – needs exact scholarship and is a mass of dates and phrases. Curious, I don't mind the loneliness now. It was ghastly at first. It's so funny to have no men coming in and out, but I hardly miss them. It's just a part of the changed conditions – and you know how adaptable we are.

But even male librarians in the Bodleian are susceptible, and Helen soon had one 'beaming all over', as well as many women friends among the Somerville staff and in the other women's colleges.

Then Cathleen Nesbitt, the well-known actress and a Belfast

friend, brought *Antony and Cleopatra* to the theatre in Oxford. Meg was very interested to hear about her, especially when Helen induced her to give a special performance for the Building Fund of Somerville. As Helen comments:

> It's something to be a popular actress. She's not only getting people (Irene Vanburgh, Mrs Patrick Campbell and Cyril Maude) but also wealthy persons with cars to run them down for the matinée. . . . There's one thing, it does you no harm in Somerville to be the source of origin of Miss Nesbitt's interest in the place, as you may imagine.

However, Helen was not content until she had proved herself scholastically, and she vacillated over which degree she should work for. She eventually decided on the Ph.D. as against the B.Litt., though she tells Saintsbury she 'hasn't much use for doctorates unless they are honorary ones, but they said it would reduce still further the standard of the B.Litt., and that I had better transfer'.

Helen always claimed she was ambitious, and her sensitive nature craved approval, so what she termed her 'blatant letters' did find their way to Meg. Quite early in her first year at Oxford she repeats two conversations:

> And even after the lecture I thought so dull, a friend met me and said with a twinkle that she had a message for me from a rather delightful big American working for the D.Phil. They were discussing dull lectures, and he said suddenly: 'But if you want to get shaken up from your very foundations, and have a rattling good time as well, you come to a lecture at twelve on Saturdays, a Miss Waddell.' She said she knew me. 'Well, tell her she has won the heart of America.'

And a more serious one:

> Darling, you're happier when you know I'm triumphant, aren't you? Miss Penrose* came to tea on Sunday and was a

*Head of Somerville.

duck. It's desperate striving work – this hand-to-mouth lecturing. But last week I had only about six pages of MS and I spoke for about an hour. It was on the jongleurs and chiefly in old French, and Miss Pope* turned up, and sat with her funny wee face screwed up like a walnut. And I quailed. But at lunch she only said: 'I wish your lectures had been put on the French list as well as the English, and they should have been.' And I knew I was received.

Then early in 1921 Helen was appointed to a lectureship under the Cassell Trust Fund and gave a course of eight lectures on 'Mime in the Middle Ages'. Her long letter about the first lecture reflects much of what contributed to her later, much more important, achievements as a lecturer.

9, Keble Road,
Oxford.
1921.

Darling,

I'm drunk with success. This place has its faults – but, Lord, it's generous in praise. Miss Moberly was there, though I didn't know it – that's the head of St Hilda's, you remember – and stayed behind to tell me what she thought of it. She just glowed upon me, said it was an immense success, and that she had enjoyed every minute of it. 'You went a little too fast for notes, but I was glad you did. I'd have hated you to miss any of it.' Talk about apathy: they were a bit shy and constrained at first, but before I'd done with them I could have them simply shouting with laughter, and faith I laughed myself.

But Peggy, Peggy – the night before I took a sudden fit of writing and wrote furiously and well till about half-past eleven; went to bed, and saw the lectures rolling out like a ribbon before me– no end of ideas, good ones too. Went to sleep about three – but in really fierce enjoyment. But nothing could help that queer breathlessness half-way down – like when you're half into the sea for the first time, and it's cold.

*Principal of Lady Margaret Hall.

But I faced them somehow – a good big room, but easy to speak in and full of caps and gowns. Thank heaven Miss Penrose was away for the weekend: she came, the lamb, to say how sorry she was and would I read it to her by herself? And Miss Lorimer had to lecture herself: but Miss Pope came, and Miss Spens, the English tutor from L.M.H. and Miss Rooke from St Hilda's (English don). I met her yesterday and she told me it was a 'wonderful' lecture. 'How do you do it?' And Maude tells me she is hearing extravagant praise from every side. Peggy, she does love me. She is just nearly hugging me with pride and joy, and made me tell her the whole lecture from beginning to end, and listened with her eyes dancing. Miss Young forgot the lecture, to her wrath – you know her funny little critical delight – but said with a twinkle that certainly my brief career in Oxford was meteoric in brilliance.

I suppose there will be a nemesis for this, but oh it's good while it lasts! Miss Pope who has no literary quality whatever, but really immense knowledge, told me it was 'most suggestive' – the one thing I feared it was not. And Miss Moberly has asked me to come to her for tea – that she wants to know me. Peggy, I think it's the funny orator's streak in our Daddy – and luckily I can just manage to fill the room with one's voice about the chanting pitch, just loud enough for the resonance you don't get in talking. I had an end bit about the survival of the Mime – Harlequin and Columbine, Punchinello and the Fool – and I swung off to 'I Pagliacci', which is coming here in a week's time – 'Remember while you watch it, the most sophisticated, diamond-cut, technically flawless of all operas, that it's the immemorial setting for the immemorial tragi-comedy – the woman and the lover, the husband and the fool: that

> "The voice you hear this passing night was heard
> In ancient days of Emperor and clown." '

Nearly all the good things in it came to me the last night, about Greek tragedy being the libretto of an opera, of which the score had vanished: the music to which Sophocles set his famous dancing measure – for he was a great *maître de ballet* as well as a tragic poet – being only another of 'the lost voices of Hellas'! Petronius Arbiter, the Aubrey Beardsley of the Roman decadence: Nero as the great amateur, with the dying regret '*Qualis artifex peres*!' 'What an artist dies in me!' to make the legend '*teres atque rotundus*'. Someday I'm going to do Nero's life as the amateur artist. I did it briefly for them, the legend 'moving from strength to strength of comedy' till one man laid his head upon his arms and laughed in sheer collapse.

And somehow it has brought me everything – brought me back Maude. She told me last night that I'd been all the success that she had ever hoped, and that they really loved me. I think she just took me for granted, you know, and being preoccupied, never bothered to take any trouble with one of whom she was sure. She said something like that last night. I was dead tired, a sort of reaction – and somehow she was the caressing Maude that you so seldom see. *Now* I can do without for a year.

Dear Peggy, it's a *blatant* letter, but you'll understand. It is so lovely to '*faire la roue*' with the peacocks, when one so frequently feels like a moulting hen. . . . I couldn't write yesterday. I was so utterly done. But it will never be so difficult again.

Much, much love
your
HELEN

P.S. If *only* I could get home for Hallowe'en! Miss Rooke told me that her best student, a third year, said it was the best lecture she had ever heard in Oxford. It's ridiculous, of course, but it's very grateful to the ear.

CHAPTER IV

Holiday in Italy

In the spring of 1921 Helen and Miss Lorimer, a History don at Somerville, spent the Easter vacation in Italy.

It was the first time Helen had travelled in Europe: her excitement and interest speak for themselves, spilled out, as always, to Meg, and starting from their arrival in Venice in Holy Week:

> Bun darling, if you were here it would make it real. Just now it cannot be really me. It's about half-past five and the sun has just gone behind the funny rough-tiled roofs opposite, and I could throw a bun into the green water of the Grand Canal. This street ends in the Canal, and is a sort of stand for gondolas. They come in and out all day long through little slim trees stuck in the water to make stalls for them, like horses, and they are slender and black and romantic; but if one is poor one goes in a dreadful little fat steamer that roars up and down the Grand Canal. Last night we came from Milan by moonlight about seven and were determined to bust and arrive in a gondola, but a little voluble man, sent by the *Padrona* to meet us, insisted on the steamer, which finally threw us off at a landing-stage, after which we were panted through innumerable dark lanes and across tiny canal bridges, me carrying a satchel of books and a large rucksack and my big coat. Only sensible reflection *en route* being relief that I had not added two volumes of my very solid Browning to books suitable to Venice and Italian atmosphere. Had been regretting him ever since leaving Oxford, but now regretted him no more. Finally arrived; panted up innumerable stairs to the Pensione which is the top flat of an enormous house, and fell with joy into two comfortable, immaculate rooms, with low broad windows and

armchairs and a view of the Grand Canal, and a marble palace which must be about fifteenth century if not older.

There's the strangest smell, half eastern, a mixture of sea-weed – for the sea-tides run through Venice – and maybe a faint suspicion of canal not quite purged by aforesaid tide – and warmth, and pleasant things being fried in quite agreeable oil. I'll never cease mourning that you are not here. Venice *is* eastern, and St Mark's positively barbaric. Anything less like our sombre western cathedrals you cannot imagine. At its best it glows like a sea shell, marble tinted pale pink and yellow and veined with blue, endless domes and sculptures of angels perching or winged, and climbing up to our Lord on the topmost pinnacle. There against the sky they look as if a breath of wind would blow them away, and lower down a blaze of mosaics, pictures of the Ascension, another of the bringing of St Mark's body from Alexandria to Venice, blue and crimson, but above all gold.

We went out to see St Mark's by moonlight last night, after dinner, and both of us being fair complexioned, were gazed at by every man we met with immense interest, which made the way to the Piazza – which is circuitous and full of unexpected glimmering canals – positively Byronic in atmosphere. The Piazza when we got there was one blaze of electric light, which drove the moon out of the sky, but when we got to the end of it and stood in front of the Doge's Palace with two steps only down to the sea and strange blue silhouettes of palaces across the canal, we were content.

This morning by the most incredible luck we strolled into the Cathedral in time for the Holy Thursday washing of the Apostles' Feet, and beheld the Archbishop of Venice, gold mitre and all, kneeling in turn before twelve old beggarmen with a copper basin and attended by his clergy with silver jugs and towels, and washing every one. He really washed them: I saw him scrub, and at the end – he being corpulent and elderly – he was red in the face and had to be helped up and down by the aforesaid clergy. He had previously exhausted himself by preaching a terrific sonorous Italian sermon, which

I could with pleasure have shortened, as I was balancing on a very small and rickety chair to see above the heads of the crowd. Had also the joy of seeing a procession of the Host, headed by a crucifix of our Lord draped in purple – every crucifix is shrouded now till Easter Sunday – and four huge candles the size of broom handles. The Host itself was carried with immense reverence by the Cardinal Archbishop – six bishops pacing before him, and himself under a magnificent gold canopy held by four men. When he reached the altar where the Host was to be laid, and where the canopy could not follow him, an attendant priest helped out with the most preposterous gold umbrella and held it over the Archbishop and Host till it reached its destination. It surely is the Eastern idea of sovereignty. But it was for the Host not for the Archbishop, as he was allowed to walk away without either umbrella or canopy.

This afternoon we took a sort of preliminary scamper through the Doge's Palace – gold ceilings, paintings by Tintoretto and Titian and Paul Veronese. Senate Room. Council Room. Room of the Council of Ten. Room of the Three Inquisitors – and finally the dungeons – cold dank narrow passages in the stone wall, with here and there an opening that you must stoop to go through, into a room a few feet square. They were in pitch darkness, no windows, except when the electric light was switched on for the visitors, and at first I thought these black openings were like manholes in a tunnel – never dreamt they were the prison. They broke their spirit first with darkness and then with torture, but the torture instruments were destroyed at the fall of the Republic about a hundred years ago. And they were 'political prisoners', not criminals. And then you open a door and come straight into the great court, blazing with light, and great marble figures of gods round it, and the delicate lightness of the columned arches, and thank God you don't live in the fifteenth century. It is the combination of the two things – the perfect sensuous imagination of beauty, and that dank cruel horror existing side by side. . . .

To Meg.

Venice
Sunday, April 3rd 1921

. . . I wish you were with us now, but I rather think you and I will come to Italy alone. We want the same things and like the same foolish idle ways. Miss Lorimer is a dear and she'd do anything you wanted, but you know us – if we throw out a half-tentative suggestion and it doesn't root, we don't pursue it. For which reason I am leaving Venice without taking a gondola and drifting across miles of lagoon to a little far away island of cypresses with only a monastery upon it – San Francesco del Deserto – where St Francis of Assisi lived for a while after he came back from the East. In one way I'm glad I haven't gone, for it will always be with me – that silent spot like an Isle of the Dead, in that waste of shining mother-of-pearl that is really what the lagoons look like at sunset. One sees it for miles because there are so few trees in Venice. And the mournful green of the cypresses makes one think of the old Renaissance trick of planting roses against their darkness for a parallel of life and sweetness in the shadow of death. Venice is the sea-witch of cities, and the sea *is* her lover. And the very things she makes are like precious stones. The ships of Venetian glass – and it's all either a riot of colour and light and pigeons whirring in the clear air and a babel of languages, like the Piazza – or else languorous and silent like the Barcarolle music – down the little green waterways – when the gondoliers sing. I suppose it's ordinary street-catches, but the cadences are really of operas like the *Miserere*. And then you remember St Francis of the Desert, away out in the lagoon, waiting with its cypress trees for a change of heart and a quiet end.

Someday I'll write to you about Torcello. And someday, please God, you and I will go there together. You take a funny little steamboat from Venice that is called affectionately '*vaporetto*', 'the little steam' – and the 'little steam' deposits you at Burano, some miles away in the lagoon and pants away again to Venice. Then you barter with a gondolier and he takes you across a stretch of water to a waste of land bare and brown like moorland, just above the level of the sea – and finds an inlet like a river mouth and drifts slowly down it. It's like coming into an enchanted land, with all around you a great waste of water, and this strange level reach of moorland held by magic above the sea. You drift past a tiny farmhouse or two, and orchards of peach blossom, and above the water's edge blackthorn shining like a white fire, and reflected in the canal below. And suddenly you're at a little landing-stage with stretches of green grass and a house or two, and under the walls of a great old church that has been there for about a thousand years. They built it, the people who fled from the Lombardy plain when the Lombards surged down from the Alps and sacked their cities; it's the old Roman civilisation taking its last stand in the marshes of the lagoons where the Goths wouldn't follow them – and from that flight came Venice, and the sovereignty of the sea. This is old Venice, and of the houses there isn't one left. And the lagoons lie on either side of the grassy paths that once were streets, and the air is incredibly wild and sweet. It blew in and out of the old church, so unlike the heavy sleeping weight of San Marco, that seems molten of incense and gold – and it's a hard heart that wouldn't pray there.

The old stiff mosaics are on the wall, still blazing with gold and green stones they're made with, young, stern angels standing about Our Lord and somehow they speak to your heart the way Titian never could no matter what he paints in the way of Madonnas, or even Tintoretto, though I've a copy of one Tintoretto you must see. Christ going to Calvary, a winding road and on the lower bend of the curve in the foreground of the picture the two thieves under their crosses and the soldiers: you take in nothing but them at first; and then on the higher road . . . you see a figure bowed under a cross straining uphill, with a faint light on it, and it dawns on you that it is Christ. The whole picture is sharp with the arms of the crosses jagged into the dull sky, and there's a dreary uncertain light in the sky – but it's all shadowy, only for the sharp angles of the cross. It is ten times more real than if the centre of the picture was Christ fainting under His cross the way it usually is in prints.

I must stop. I've straggled away from Torcello. I think the whole effect of that old church was the feeling that you knew the temper of faith that made things like the Athanasian Creed. But there was an arched doorway beside it, and through it you saw framed in the dark arch the whole magic level of the lagoon and the silent land, with the sprays here and there of young, green thorn trees, and the light of a peach tree in flower, close at hand. I've never seen anything like it, the tenderness and the light and the strangeness of it. You know nearly every place has an association – you can think of it in terms of something else. But Torcello was like the kingdom of heaven. . . .

P.S. It's something like O'Shaughnessy's:

> 'How far away among the hazy lands
> That float beneath the rising sun's new rim
> Is that enchanted country.'

To Meg.

Venice
Easter Monday 1921

. . . I bought a panama hat, just like the big floppy one you used to like, and got it for 80 lire, which in the present blessed rate of exchange is just 11/–. Once you're here, living is dirt cheap, and I hanker after you dreadfully. . . . The fellowship won't be decided till next term – I hear there's a very good Oxford person up for it: and I can't see how in any probability I'll ever have a chance – you see, one isn't even allowed to apply till the thing has been thrown open, and they aren't likely to turn down their own for a vague mass of outsiders perhaps no better. But there's always the chance. Anyhow Miss Penrose said herself that those exam reports were the best she'd ever had. . . . In some ways we aren't lucky, but in other ways we are. Sometimes when I think what it would be like to be alive and not have you – somehow you're like a house with a sunny garden to me, the house with all sorts of homely warm comfortableness in it: another sunny garden for our holidays together. Sometime you and I *must* come to Italy. Both Maude and Miss Lorimer like guide books, so do I. But you and I would be in a gondola down the Grand Canal, and not bother whose palace we were passing, but just watch the old stained marble and the green waters.

To Professor Saintsbury.

Venice
30th March, 1921

Thursday morning. This letter is a little drunk, but it was written in the middle of the night.

> 'Because all words, though culled with choicest art,
> Failing to give the tithe of the sweet,
> Wither beneath the palate.'

Take these flowers. They will be withered too when they come to you: but just now the violet is surely enough, and the other – is it samphire? – is salt with the sea. I could find nothing in Venice to send you. But today I gathered these on the island of Torcello – *Venice antica*, as the gondoliers called it – where the streets are little grassy paths with lagoons on either side, and for houses there were peach trees in blossom, and only the cathedral left with a pavement like the body of heaven at sunset. It was a day like the colour of your moonstone, and the doors of the church were wide open, and the faith of it – the faith that knew the taking of the manhood into God. I found the violets beside the wall, and the samphire at the edge of one of the little paths close to the sea edge, and beside it a blackthorn in blossom. I do not think I will ever see the like of Torcello again. Torcello is a new dream, that it had not entered into my heart to conceive. I know now that I have been in one of the 'hazy lands that float beneath the rising sun's new rim'. And these are the grasses of it, that you may take seisin.

Your
HELEN

To Professor Saintsbury.

Rimini
April 9th, 1921

My Lord,
I did not write from Ravenna, because it was not ours. For the Pine Forest has been burned, and the trees that are left were thin and very sorrowful. And for the rest, I think the sixth century is perhaps the one of the hundred years we missed. We have not much part with Justinian and Theodora. If she had been Thaïs, I could have loved her, and the blaze of the mosaic in San Vitale would not have distressed me, even at the altar rails. But it was her cruelty I cannot endure. Besides, I knew I was coming to Rimini.

I'm in a little island of candlelight in the middle of a huge tiled floor – and solitary, for I seem to have caught a chill, and so luxuriously had dinner in my room. I couldn't bring myself to head this letter 'Palace Hotel, Rimini'. It's bitter seeing the name printed in huge letters as the train comes in to the station. But there are the ramparts still, and the orange sails on the river, and the arches of the bridge, and San Marino a great way off, looking down at you from its towers. And – the Tempio di Malatesta.

I am haunted by them tonight – not Francesca, nor Paolo, but the heads of that accursed house. I want you sometime to tell me the story of Sigismond and Isotta, for if ever two flaunted their loves before Gods and men, it was they. The interwoven monogram is everywhere, and the tombs are as massive as Sigismond's elephants and as rich as Isotta's rose. It is certainly the Temple of the Malatesta, it's even a Temple *to* the Malatesta, and the arrogance and the hardness and the pride of life of it has taken possession of me this night. In its way it's magnificent: but – I am perversely haunted by Tintoretto's *Ariadne and Bacchus*, which is the very heart of Venice for me. It's in the Ducal Palace and the sun blazes on it, but it has only mellowed it, and Bacchus stands knee-deep in the cool green sea, with vine leaves and grapes for a girdle, and a boy's beseeching in his eyes. But the light of it is the light of Venice, not like these barbarians of Malatesta, overlaid with enough of the Renaissance to make them more formidable. This is an absurd place, but it's the first time I've actually come up against the Renaissance tyrant, and I'll swear he is abroad in Rimini yet.

Mantua
Sunday night

I was too tired to finish, and we came on by an early train here. I am haunted by Venice, and I know I'm going back. The rest of Italy is political and one crosses Piazzi Garabaldis and Via Cavours without end. But in Venice you walk in *Calles* of the Holy Apostles, and cross the Bridge of Honest Ladies, and San Marco's lion seems to walk beside you like a dog. It's true that at first Venice was too wholly what I'd hoped that one almost suspected stage-managing. But after seven days one is her slave, the more that she dares to be a little comical. Nothing can spoil Venice, not even the U.S.A. motor-launch tearing down in the morning for its mail, instead of waiting for the peaceful official gondola. Two things I have kept against the time I return again, Venice in a gondola at night and Sàn Francesco of the Desert, a solitary island of cypresses, waiting out in the lagoon like the remembrance of death.

Helen and Miss Lorimer stayed four days in Paris on their way home and their reaction shows what a great success the holiday had been:

From Paris
April 1921

. . . Paris! Henry James talks about its light at night: 'a twinkling grin set on the face of pleasure', and that's Paris all day long. I never was in a city so gay and friendly and kindly, and for all I've seen of it no wickedness but a kind of innocent naughtiness. *Rianté* is the word for it, especially now that it's April, and warm sun in between the showers. Today we climbed the tower of Notre Dame, and the sun showered itself over Paris, and the wind blew, a kind of gay rollicking wind, and the old tower hummed with it; a happy *bourdon* with a big tree, and beside us the old *Penseur* gargoyle sat with his chin in his hands and his wise gargoyle face in a sort of sardonic grin, wide for all Paris below him. Must send you a p.c. of him. But the shops, and the hats, and the shoes – gold shoes with buckles like a dragonfly's wings, set up peacock-tail fashion. Wait till *we* come! I've bought my summer hat, black, with a chain round the edge of the brim of flame-coloured japonica, very tiny flowers. And I've bought a hat for Mary that I'm dying to see her in. I'll bring it when I come. Tell her. I got it and mine in the great *Bon Marché* – which is anything but its name, but much the nicest shop we've seen, and really much cheaper than at home, thanks to the exchange.

And we've had four nights' opera, at the very top of the huge opera house, which is like the heart of Paris, mighty and domed, with a foyer and stairs like a Renaissance Palace, and in between the acts all the *grandes toilettes de Paris* stream out and go round and round the foyer like the 'Grand Old Duke of York', in threes and twos.

CHAPTER V

Aftermath of Oxford

Helen did not return to Oxford to complete the required terms of residence for her doctorate. In spite of Oxford's manifest appreciation of her, she instinctively backed away from academic restrictions and the enclosed atmosphere of university work. Fortunately her applications for posts were unsuccessful: her scholarship was more than adequate but she lacked the necessary practical experience.

In the meantime she kept herself out of debt by correcting immense piles of school and university examination papers. All she wanted was financial security to give her peace to write, but, as she lived on her emotions, on her heart more than on her head, she never truly adjusted herself to the practical pressures of living, nor to her own temperament and her amazing talents. Nevertheless she had the courage and determination to abandon Oxford and find lodgings in London, trusting to freelance lecturing and uncertain literary jobs to cover her modest expenses until the books in her mind, already promised by her creative power, should be given to the world.

Helen reveals her state of nervous indecision to Saintsbury as well as to Meg. In August 1922, the former is told:

> I sit here all day, mowing down exam papers at the rate of sixty per day. Thanks to the Dublin fracas they came to me two weeks late. I was in Dublin one night and there was sniping all round the hotel, but otherwise nothing – except dinner with very nice Paul Henry! He's just had a picture accepted by the Luxembourg. I'm horribly afraid that artists and journalists are more my sort than academic people. *You* aren't academic. Tell me about the 'address'. I've seen no

papers for months – and found you, of all places, in the *Daily Sketch*, as the G.O.M. of criticism. I contemplated the paragraph for a few minutes, (I being in the train), and thought how very odd it was that I should be

Your
HELEN

And by November 1921 when she was settled in her lodgings in St Edmund's Terrace in St John's Wood, London, she tells him:

I have never been so happy. Great Babylon has me bewitched. I cannot write anything yet, but the desire to write that has been dead in me for two years has come back, and perhaps the capacity will come. I've never felt so alive. I'm drowned with work, and it doesn't so much as tire me. And the young man for whom you always had an affection is here, and my slave. And there is a rather charming American too.

Meantime you have your
HELEN

At the same period she was discussing more practical problems with Meg, such as the possibility of a post at Bedford College:

I was talking to Miss Kempson (Dean of Residence, Bedford) about next year. I stay in London. I had a charming letter from Miss Pope, asking me to give herself and Miss Lorimer a week-end at Oxford. I think I'll go sometime in November.

Craig, the decent Registrar there, is trying to get my eight terms reduced to the five that I have already done. . . . It will save me £12 anyhow, and if he manages his other, I'll never have to go back to Oxford at all. Glory be! Life is good. These London dusks, with the lamps lit and a big red sun going down in the smoke – and yet on Saturday night an odd thing happened. I was coming home from shopping, just in that dark, with the streets at their 'lifeiest', and – ah, you know the excitement of a crowd, and the way innumerable voices, and a kid crying, and the honking of taxis, all blend into a sort of Wagner chorus. And suddenly just for a moment I was at the back of the Mourne Mountains, at the door of a wee earth house, looking over the slopes of heather and the wet bog, in the same twilight, with the sun just down. But, ah, the quiet of it. And I was watching for my man coming home, and there was nobody but the two of us in the world. Maybe it did happen – about two thousand years ago. But Peggy, can't you imagine how queer it was – and how the streets suddenly became horrible to me?

I feel as if those two years in Oxford were a bad dream. There are moments here in London, when you feel the same amazed delighted security as the first time you find you're really swimming, but I don't grudge the Oxford years, after all, think of the people.

I don't want to badger you to write; but any time you have – it doesn't matter *what* you say. *Anything* about Killy or Magherally is what my heart feeds on.

An unpublished and undated poem seems palpably connected with this dream. It was written some time after Helen had been to Kilmacrew and had refused to marry an ardent young lover while walking in the Mountains of Mourne, but had been seriously tempted to accept his proposal:

I shall not go to Heaven when I die,
But if they let me be,
I think I'll take a road I used to know
That goes by Shere-na-garagh and the sea.
And all day breasting me the winds will blow,
And I'll hear nothing but the peewits' cry
And the waves talking in the sea below.

I think it will be winter when I die
For no one from the North could die in spring –
And all the heather will be dead and grey;

And the bog-cotton will have blown away,
And there will be no yellow on the whin.

But I shall smell the peat,
And when it's almost dark I'll set my feet
Where a white track goes glimmering to the hills,
And see far up a light . . .
Would you think Heaven could be so small a thing
As a lit window on the hills at night?
And come in stumbling from the gloom,
Half-blind, into a firelit room,
Turn, and see you.
And there abide.

If it were true,
And if I thought that they would let me be,
I almost wish it were tonight I died.

Helen herself records that: 'In the morning I remembered and wrote it down. And that day, or the day after, I wrote the first few paragraphs of *The Wandering Scholars*.'

In spite of shortage of money and unsuccessful applications for university posts, the atmosphere of London stimulated Helen from the moment of arrival, and especially after weekends in Oxford, where she was received by the heads of the Women's Colleges with pleasure and a flattering rivalry among them as they renewed their efforts to lure her back to them:

> I was at Oxford from Thursday till Sunday, and, oh so glad to be back in London. I had to talk steadily and continuously for about two days. They want awfully to renew the fellowship, but the worst of it is they've advertised it. So they are summoning a special committee on me sometime next week, and may possibly end by giving me a special Fellowship for a year. . . . But it was very soothing to the mind to feel oneself a bone between two colleges.

Although inevitably, but temporarily, depressed by each successive rejection by London colleges too – Bedford, Westfield and King's – for the same reason of lack of experience in administration and teaching, Helen could still dramatise her interviews with humour and a mixture of relief and self-criticism: 'I wouldn't appoint myself,' she tells Meg when faced with a resident post at King's that required the holder to act as Warden over the girls as well as tutor and lecturer. Her reaction to the selection committee is typical:

> . . . The council is over, and I don't think I've got it, though they were as nice as they could be. And anyhow just before I went in I heard Miss Levett, the Vice-Principal of St Hilda's in Oxford was in for it, so I gave up the ghost. But what really dished me was their very first question. 'Are you prepared to become Warden of the hostel as well as Tutor?' And the surprise of it got the truth out of me. I just said: 'No.' Do you think I was mad? Of course when I first thought of the job, I had no idea one had to be Warden: I thought they wanted residence, but that there was a Warden already. There was an awfully nice chairman, Canon Barnes of Westminster, thin and middle-aged, with eyes that smiled at you even before he spoke, so that you found yourself talking as if there were nobody else there. I just asked him if it wouldn't mean eating up one's whole life, tutor and general adviser all day at King's, Warden for over 300 girls at night? (At Bedford there are only 90 and Miss Tuke has a Bursar and a Resident Tutor and two resident staff as well as a matron.) And he hesitated a moment and then smiled. 'Yes, it would eat you up.' Add to that, four lectures a week. Then they said: 'Would you be content with the very elementary lecturing involved in this post?' Meaning that you do the pass classes and the odd jobs of the English School. To which I said: 'I would not.' Sudden strangled chuckle from Dr Barker. I felt in my secret soul that I was behaving exactly as he had thought I would. They asked me all manner of questions, about experience and responsibility, worst of all, the *awful* and I

think unfair one: 'Does this post really attract you?' 'No – except that I like girls, and would be ready to try it.' I was mad – but something subliminal in me got on top and I was helpless. You know how the things you have argued yourself into believing suddenly melt in emergency. I had drugged myself into thinking I wouldn't mind responsibility, that it would be good for me. . . . Well, it just vanished. I can't repent it, for somehow I think one must tell the truth about one's self. I couldn't believe it when I got into the street – it was an odd ten minutes of sheer naked truth. And I cursed myself for a fool, but something obstinate in me rejoiced. It was like the night I dreamed I was going to be married – and woke in a panic, the slow sudden relief. And at the very end Dr Barker drawled out: 'Well, no matter how this appointment goes, I think we are all agreed that we want you at King's in some capacity. We'd be honoured to have you as lecturer, if opportunity comes.' So I'm to hear from them in a day or two. Canon Barnes got up: 'I think before you go we all want to thank you for the absolute frankness with which you have treated us.'

Professor Spurgeon saw me *en route*: 'Well, I hope you don't get it. And you won't – far too young.' Honestly, it's a job for forty-three. Ten years away, I might, and probably ten years away I will. But meantime. . . .

In May 1922 Helen was stunned and horrified by a letter offering her the post of headmistress of The Victoria College for Girls – her own school in Belfast. Meg supported her refusal to bury herself for years in an administrative job that had only one attraction for her – proximity to Kilmacrew.

CHAPTER VI

Paris

Fortunately in the autumn of that same year Professor Saintsbury gave Helen an eulogistic reference to pass on to the Committee of Lady Margaret Hall, which must undoubtedly have influenced their decision to award her the Susette Taylor Travelling Fellowship for two years. So her problems were solved, and, with a high heart she went to Paris to continue her medieval researches for the *Wandering Scholars* in the *Bibliothèque Nationale*.

She plunged into her work, and was too absorbed to have time for other interests or other people. Indeed she fled from the atmosphere of an Anglo-American Club where she resided on first arrival, being unable to keep pace with its chatter and friendly sociabilities. She settled down with a congenial French couple who refused to speak anything but French with her, and taught her German as well. She also found 'a rather wonderful Russian girl who knows medieval Latin and scholastic philosophy, and I go and talk three hours a week'. It is not long before she is telling Meg that 'the Sorbonne is open and I'm going to a lecture of Faral's* once a week. Mercifully I no longer feel as if water were roaring in my ears when addressed in rapid French. I'm even screwing up my courage to send him Miss Pope's letter of introduction instead of waiting till after Christmas. It is my own subject, medieval Latin. I feel quite hollow inside, because I know all these people and go skating around on nice polished floors, and never see anybody who knew me before, and nothing matters in life but getting the book written. But it's a satisfaction that I'm in honour bound to Lady Margaret Hall to do that book.'

*Faral: well-known expert on medieval Latin.

However, she did make one lasting friendship through an introduction given her by Miss Lorimer, to a French doctor of medicine. His name was Albert Vaudremer, an outstanding personality of high repute in Paris for his researches at the Hôpital Pasteur, and for the services he gave, often voluntarily, to the sick and needy.

In 1924 Helen collapsed with a bad bout of laryngitis and influenza: he came to her rescue, whisked her into the Pasteur hospital and looked after her. All through her two years in Paris she spent most of her spare time with his wife and family; and before and after the Second World War Dr Vaudremer and his daughter Nicole exchanged visits with her in Paris and in London.

To Professor Saintsbury Helen usually writes about her work, asking for and receiving critical comments from him. Occasionally she writes more personally, and in one letter repeats a dream* she had of herself as Héloise, when old and Abbess of the Paraclete, after Abelard's death. Héloise overhears one of the novices after her lesson muttering: '*C'est toujours le théologie d'Abelard.*' Apart from dreams, ideas for her subsequent novel must have been taking shape in her conscious mind even then, for she tells him: 'I am back at B.N. to find out if that amazing dirge for Abelard – do you know it? "*Requiescat a labore, Doloroso et amore*" is genuine, or at least twelfth century, and not a sentimental forgery. It seems too good to be true.' (In a later letter she records her delight at finding it was written in the twelfth century.)

She slowly grew to feel at home in Paris, especially after she had found a minute flat in the Rue de Passy. Among the friends whose company she enjoyed most were several impassioned admirers. One young man, particularly determined to marry her, was an American: he came over from the United States obsessed with the idea, and though he succeeded in rousing Helen's compassion to a dangerous degree, he had to return alone. Always her deep fear of marriage was stronger than herself, yet she

*See p. 220.

believed and hoped she would one day meet her ideal – Abelard. And to Meg she poured out the whole incident:

Russell left yesterday morning at ten. It has been really terrible, and yet I've seldom liked him so much. It's a pity.

I seem to have spent eternity dining, lunching, drinking champagne, driving in the Bois, watching Montmartre at two o'clock in the morning – real Montmartre this time, a kind of Comus rout, and all the time Russell like a grim old enchanter coaxing, coaxing, with awful bursts of fury. Till at last – the last night, I broke down and cried in the taxi, luckily we were in moonlight woods in the Bois, and it didn't matter. I'd been wanting to cry for days, so it was a great satisfaction to me and I believe it saved Russell's reason. For he had to forget and just be fatherly and petting, and anyhow it proved that I wasn't what he called me, a fiend and not a woman. I can't believe it's me that these things happen to. The last three days with him have been too like grand opera. Then came one quiet clear spring afternoon. Russell about as exhausted as myself, and we drove and drove in an open car through woods and dim pleasant country, spring mists on the river – to Versailles and home by St Germain, where Henry of Navarre had a 'pavillion', and we had tea on a wonderful terrace with a sheer drop to the valley of the Seine, and all Paris like a grey shell, and a luminous sunset and we gossiped, just drifting like boats down stream. Then back to Paris for dinner, and another row – the worst yet. I think this time he knows it's hopeless. He told me he had counted everything on this visit to Paris. I came home and shivered till daylight and then slept. Just wakened to remember that he left at ten. And I wondered would it be any good, just to do one thing of ordinary kindness – go and see him off, with no time for a row. It took the taxi hours, it seemed, and I couldn't make up my mind till the last minute whether I'd really go into the Gare du Nord or not. 10 to 10. Got out. Stopped at barrier. '*Mais si vous plait, m'sieur, je veux dire Bon Voyage à mon ami*' – and being French they beamed on me, and let me through.

Looked through two first-class blocks – no Russell – then glanced out and saw big solitary figure on the platform, looking at nothing, awfully dejected. So I hopped down from the train almost on top of him. And I think it was the best thing I've ever done in my life. He took nothing out of it but just kindness, like a cold hand on a hot head. And he went away, still very grim, but comforted. I came home and slunk into bed, throat – cough and all the rest of it. But oh the peace! Surely this will be the end!

Helen certainly had an understanding friend in Professor Saintsbury: his age and his outsize beard were protective symbols, and her own security had no need of reserve or restriction. Yet the artificiality of their imaginary 'Samarkand' correspondence did strike her after a time, and in 1924, while she was still in Paris, she tells Meg:

I was awfully glad to get Saintsbury's letter. I wrote to him, but I had a feeling that it had all gone hollow – the bubble pricked with the 'sharpness of death'. And yet I knew how deep my feeling for him had gone, apart from play-acting, and suddenly felt empty. Then came this: 'As usual you have said what nobody else could say as you could say it. But I won't answer till I have your Paris address. Benedictions. G.S.' And you feel as if the old things were still with you; you know one's terror of a change that goes to the roots.

So the correspondence between Helen and Professor Saintsbury continued without inhibition:

I think I wrote you a very dim letter last time. Odd things have happened inside me since. I suddenly discovered that I *like* being by myself. It's this way, I can't manage work and people together. Someone once said that I never did anything decent unless I had been driven to get my excitement out of the work instead of people. And this is true. My present content is partly because Paris all by itself is a good shadow-show; and chiefly because of the '*scholares vagantes*'. Just now I am doing an amusing thing, reading nothing but the things they read. I found to my disgrace that I have taken Virgil for granted, ever since I was sixteen. It was a revelation to come back to him, with some living in between. And I know now why Alcuin cried over Dido, and Odo saw the brood of serpents in the porcelain vase.

Also, I came upon the *Copa*.* For a foolish moment, I hoped it was yours. Anyhow, I've translated it. May I send it to you when it's finished? It's so contemporary: or perhaps nearer the very end of the nineteenth century, but younger than anything I know of them. But there are scores of things I want to talk about. Yesterday, after a morning of the De Arte Amandi† I came out into the Avenue de L'Opéra. And suddenly I realised why we speak of the 'Latin' nations. There was no transition. And I thought with a sudden hankering, of Great Russell St or Piccadilly itself, for that matter. It may be your 'accepted hells beneath': but they *are* beneath. And if we accept them and go down into them, at least we call them hell. Or else 'the heaven that leads men to this hell'. It's very good, after a long morning's saunter past French print shops to come back to the Sonnets. I don't think I need tell you at this time of day that I am not a Puritan. And I *like* Donne's 'full nakedness! All joys are due to thee'. I am inconsistent. Perhaps it's because this art is so aware that it just took off its clothes a minute ago.

Write to me. It is as if I had come to Paris at last, and for the first time. The *Quartier* is so Americanised, demoralised, and I sickened in it. And Passy is still in the unfashionable strata – a little country town – '*La ville de Passy*', one of the little shops calls it. I am haunted by St Peter Damian tonight. Rémy de Gourmont‡ says that '*le latin mystique*' is the one thing that '*convient à notre immense fatigue*'. My love to you.

*The Copa: one of a collection of early poems attributed to Virgil.

†'Courtly Love' – which inspired the first half of the *Roman De La Rose*.

‡Essayist, novelist and critic, associated with the Symbolist Movement. Died 1915.

This letter has said nothing but trivial things but they are all of them inadequate ways of saying that

Your
HELEN

But it is Meg who has the last letter about Helen's work in Paris before she returned to London in 1925:

I wish you were here to tell you about this work, it's getting better and better. I've often wondered if there was anything behind the paganism of the *Carmina*; how the Middle Ages could write anything so completely unconscious of morals and the whole system of Christian thinking, with Venus really in the apple orchard, and Bacchus in the tavern. But two days ago I began to read Bernard Silvestris, who was one of the most popular masters in the XIIth century in France. Nobody reads him now, though in his own day they called him the greatest of the Platonists. He is a poet-philosopher, like Shelley. His imagination takes your breath. He's describing Nature in search of Urania – the two together are to create Man. Urania is the goddess – Soul of the universe, you see, but Nature can find her nowhere, and there is an amazing paragraph in prose, of how Nature went seeking her through parallels and magnitudes and the circuits of the planets and the orbits of the spheres. 'From splendour to nullity he sought her, from heaven to the Kingdom of Dis: from eternity to those misshapen bodies that lie in the House of the Crab, that purer essences have denied to habitation and abandoned, shuddering.' It's ghastly, but the power of it! And, last of all, it's the intellectual counterpart, this, of the *Carmina*. And I can trace an almost immediate connection between him and the most famous of my poets – a kind of early Rabelais at Orleans.

If Bernard is not Bernard of Chartres it matters very little, except that one covets so great a piece of imaginative prose as the '*De Mundi Universitate*' for the town which of all towns in France has kept the secret of the Middle Ages, yet brought them into the current of ageless and hereditary beauty. For the rediscovery of the dignity of the human body which is in every sculpture of Chartres, of the beauty and the abiding value of 'the whole sensible appearance of things' is brought to the twelfth century as to the sixteenth by the Platonists. Bernard Silvestris in his '*De Universitate*' did for the poets and sculpture of the twelfth and thirteenth centuies what Giordano in '*Gli Heroici Furori*' did for Sidney and Spenser in Elizabethan England.

Meg, my darling, I'll never be happy till you and I go to Chartres together.

The previous year, 1924, two Belfast friends, Mrs McNeill and her daughter Jane, had taken Helen in a private car for a tour round Touraine. As usual she wrote excitedly to Meg.

Hotel de l'Univers
Tours

I know at last why people love France. I never could understand Mary Queen of Scots yearning after it, if it meant Paris. But it was in Touraine she must have spent most of her life, and her honeymoon was at a château we're going to see tomorrow. I felt the difference in one of those queer moments that make travelling worth while and that didn't come even in the forests at Fontaine where we drove on Saturday. I'd looked out of the carriage windows several times between Paris and Orleans, same flat country, uniform and green. And suddenly I looked, and saw the Loire – a great gentle expanse of water, with shallows and sand and green islets of grass, and on the further bank trees and steep-tiled houses and a grey château on the hill. It was as faded and gentle as an old colour print – an aquatint, and after that, you felt you had come to an older country, not Vogue and Monmartre and the Champs Élysées. Even the hotel is like an old French country house with shining polished wooden floors and faint pleasant colours in the curtains and the rugs, and shallow wooden stairs, and the most wonderful cooking. Tours itself is just an old country town, with a cathedral, and some old houses and wee streets that you really could shake hands across – the street of the Halberd, of the Four Winds, of the Cherry Trees, and every here and there a green gleam of the river.

It's gone cold all at once, and Jane is triumphant because in heat so fierce that I was sleeping with only a sheet she packed woollen knickers and a burberry. But it's fine, and tomorrow we drive all day. It's awfully pleasant, and sometimes I run out by myself, and then it's adventures like the *Gentleman of France* (Stanley Weyman). We went to High Mass in the Cathedral today, and Mrs McNeill knelt and bowed to the altar like a good Papist. I do love her, more every day. When I talk to her about the Middle Ages, she listens as if I were the Ancient Mariner. I was describing Chartres, where so many of my great bishops lived, and since then it's always: 'Now tell me more about Ivo.' Also, what so few people realise, she said one day: 'Helen, it's good company you keep in your work. I'd like to have the Fathers all round me like that.' Jane is really behaving awfully well. I hear a good deal of her own excellence as a traveller, till in self-defence I produced a rhyme which gets added to every day. You will read between the lines.

JANE or The Perfect Traveller

She likes to travel in the train.
She never smells an open drain.
On boats she talks to stewardesses,
And gives advice in their distresses.
She is not sick in any swell,
But only in each new hotel.
And even in Paris summer heat
She wears goloshes on her feet.

To Meg.

Touraine

. . . We were away all day, and it was very queer. You know I have never cared for the Renaissance in France – stopped liking it after the thirteenth century, always thought of it spoiling the old romances and the old chansons with Boileau and Racine and Corneille, and the balustrades and sham classic stuff at Versailles. But I saw the dawn of it today. France, just about the time Mary Queen of Scots was a young girl in it. First it was Loches for the Middle Ages at their cruelest – Louis XI (the Quentin Durward stories) with dungeons and oubliettes and dark, harsh walls and towers, all in a downpour of rain. And suddenly it cleared and the sun came out very gentle, and the trees stood with their feet in grassy shining water, and we came down a long avenue of trees to Chenonceaux. The Loire flows all round it – or a wee tributary of it; and there are moats with water lilies, and a long gallery built out on arches, with a glimmer of swaying lights from the river. It's all green and glancing like being under water, shallow enough for the sun to shine in it. Mary Queen of Scots was there, and awfully happy: and I was away by myself and suddenly 'the sense of the Past' that you and I know came on me – do you remember, in Wadham Garden, watching *Twelfth Night*? Chenonceaux is not simple, it's very ornate, elaborate chimneys and ceilings and tapestries and wonderful carved armoires, plenty of dim gold and red: but even the 'Grand Salon' was a friendly place, and the little library, with a great embrasured window to the river was like a jewel casket, and everywhere the radiance of the water. Henry II of France built it for Diane de Poitiers who was his mistress: their two initials are everywhere: but when he died, Catherine de Medici – you know the St Bartholemew Catherine – turned her out of it before Henry was in his grave almost. Even so, there isn't much of Catherine about it, much more of Diane, who was bright-haired.

I'm really pleased about today. It was a real revelation; and it has suddenly illuminated a whole century – and things like Ronsard's poetry have found a setting at last. But Mary, poor little Mary, to leave it for Holyrood and Edinburgh.

CHAPTER VII

London after Paris

So Helen returned to life in London and revelled in the peace of larger rooms in the St Edmund's Terrace house:

> I can hardly believe it's me. It doesn't seem right that anyone should be in such peace. Darling, it's all ridiculous, but you have to have wandered for about eighteen months in clubs and hotels, and lived and slept and washed and cooked in one room to feel like this. It's like your belt being too tight and suddenly loosened, only the belt is round your head. . . . Wakened on Sunday morning nice and lazy: after a bit looked at my watch – quarter past eleven. And this morning it was half past ten. I've told nobody I'm back, though I'll begin stirring tomorrow.

Helen's stirring had the instantaneous effect of sociability: 'Positively gallant letter from Gregory this morning about tomorrow's dinner . . . I think it would take very little effort to land that good whale.'

Very soon remarks about writing *The Wandering Scholars* begin to appear: 'I've begun the second chapter; "The Pagan Learning" is the first one. This will be the new lyric in the fifth century. Maude is here. I read her bits; she is awfully taken with the book.'

After a visit from Miss Lorimer, Helen wrote that: 'She thinks my book will make my name. Also she's talking about giving a dinner next term to meet the Gilbert Murrays. I did meet them once before with her, and she says Lady Murray is always asking her about me, because I seem to remind her of their girl who died in Paris when she was doing research. It nearly broke their hearts.

'But somehow nothing matters but the book.'

Yet a letter to Professor Saintsbury in the same period sounds slightly contradictory:

We had a long talk yesterday, you and I, in a window of the London Library, longest perhaps over the projected word motive '*Je n'ai pas d'amant*': but we had also a thousand things to say about *Le Lys Rouge*. Do you know that that book hurt me horribly. I am very nearly tired of love. Last night, it was one of the new men, young and rather like Symmers, from the Southern States. There is no hope or expectation in him. He knows me and explains me to myself till I almost shiver at his penetration. Last night he told me I would never love until I met a man bigger than myself – which he was good enough to say would be difficult – but that in the meantime I suffered. It's true. I do suffer. But for half a moment I could have slain him! He loves me. And I think I do him good and not evil, for there is some greatness in him, and an immense diffidence. And I don't let him kiss me. It's that that wakes the devil in love – or its god. Which, Excellency? Both I think, and the two are one. But I am tired, tired.

Dear old Gregory, he came here to see me, and stayed three mortal hours, and I showed him a divine pair of gold and ruby shoes, and he felt a gay dog – bless its innocent heart.

By March 1926, Helen is seeking new university posts as well as possible work for publishers. Patience did not come easily to her, so Meg receives almost daily letters.

No news yet about the Westfield job; it isn't in the paper yet. But I got desperate and went and saw Mr Kyllmann* of Constable's about next term. (And the fur coat was not lost on him. I do like that man.)

And he thinks he'll have something for me to do next term, after Easter. I just told him how things were, and the gap before I could get another job; and when he asked me if I had anything in my mind to write, I told him about the MSS

*Otto Kyllmann: Chairman of Constable.

in the British Museum, and the 13th-century Oxford letters. He looked awfully interested, said they sounded very promising, and finally: 'Now go home and finish your book, and I'll talk to you when you bring it to me.' So I came home stepping delicately. He says there has been a scheme in his mind for sometime, but he wants to think it out. Oh dear, it's better than County Council lecturing.

By April Helen is on the short list for the Westfield post, but once again she has to face disappointment:

I was very near it. A man has got it. It was so little teaching that did me in. They said the Head of Department must have that. But I was right about the Committee. They just fell for me. After it, I was neck and neck with this man. He was Sir Sidney Lee's* assistant with a good war record, six years lecturing and a book on the Italian Renaissance in the press. How I even got on the short list, and still more how I ran this man so close – they say it was sheer personality. Well dear, it wasn't enough, it seems.

Helen was nothing if not resilient, an optimist to the core as far as she herself was concerned: up and down, but more quickly and more permanently up. Before the month of May 1926 was out, she was writing to Meg:

Could you believe it, I now don't care? Honest, I can't understand it, but I meet condolence with a wide grin. Something just died in me, went out like a little spurt of a match. I feel as if it were the last kick of the years that the locust ate. And now I'm cheerfully discussing East London, and getting on like blazes with the footnotes. It's a thousand pities the book hadn't been out. It would have tipped the balance . . . I *must* get experience in teaching.

Helen was right not to fear the future. Her reputation as a

*Sir Sidney Lee: Shakespearian scholar, editor of the *D.N.B.*

lecturer had been made in Oxford. And Constable's had written that she might take her time as the American publisher was not coming 'just now'. She reports the fluctuations of her progress to Meg:

> The tenth century is finished. I got it through last night. Today the XIth. At this rate I'll have three weeks to do all the technical references and appendices with real care. It's awful doing details in a hurry.
>
> I've had the nicest letter from Miss Grier (Lady Margaret Hall). They're giving me £20 for six lectures, to cover travelling expenses, which after all are only 7/– a cheap day return, and any time I want I am to stay the night.

In due course the lectures started and Helen gives Meg a vivid description of the first:

> There was such a crowd that they had to move me out of the ordinary lecture-room into the 'Writing School' where the examinations are held and I almost died with panic and pride. And the morning had been so dreadful, for I had been awake from four, afraid to miss the 8.40 train because my alarm stopped in the middle of the night, and I couldn't trust it. You know the ghastly train feeling you have at that time in the morning.
>
> L.M.H. awfully kind to me but miserable about the lecture. 'Why did they put you on the first day of term? Nobody goes anywhere the first day. And Professor Gordon is on at the same time, and the whole English School is bound to go there. And, worst of all, Dr Gretton is lecturing on Aristotle, and we've had to send our history students there. . . .' But these things never play on me. I'd faced the worst when I saw Gordon was lecturing and was prepared for them! There were people waiting at the door, evidently the first lecture wasn't out. . . . Doors opened at 12.5 and crowds came out like bees in a hive. Miss Jamison* plunged for the porter at the door

*Miss Jamison: Vice-Principal of Lady Margaret Hall.

and came back bursting with elation: 'There's been standing-room only since five minutes to twelve, and they're moving you to the North School.'

But I didn't take it in till I looked through the door of North. There must have been hundreds there for the room has two wings and it was thick. The worst of it was that my pulpit was designed for a supervisor at exams rather than for oratory, and it was frightfully hard to reach both wings. As you know I carry pretty far when it's a decent hall, but yesterday was fierce. Polly comforted me by saying that I'd a bigger crowd even than the Astronomer Royal last term, and that she couldn't hear him either in the same room and the same seat.

L.M.H. burst with pride and joy and Maude had heard people talking and saying it was 'frightfully exciting'.

And I came back very limp to find a charming note from Kyllmann asking me to lunch today. But I am almost dead this morning with pure fatigue. But will brisk up and be lively at lunch.

And there's the interview on Friday. . . . After this week I'll begin to live again. At the moment it's like shooting rapids or rather catching trains all the time.

Meanwhile Helen moved from her rooms in St Edmund's Terrace to a small flat in Ormonde Terrace on the south side of Primrose Hill, with an open view of green grass, bushes and trees in which birds sang. She was entranced by the quiet and her tiny balcony where she sat and wrote undisturbed, and here she lived the six most productive years of her scholarly, creative mind.

A cheering interview with Dr Barker and Professor Reid, both of King's College, London, softened her failure to be selected for the post for East London:

They both wanted me, and both say that I am to come to King's just when I choose – take the L.M.H. Fellowship by all means and come to them when it's over, or if I don't get it to come to them this October. It sounds too good to be true. Peggy, the incredible thing is that King's is supposed to be antifeminine and Dr Barker too. But here they are standing round and saying they'll be honoured. And they haven't seen a bally testimonial or anything – just me talking. Sometimes I think it's a dream and I'll wake up to find myself saying 'yes please' for a job in a school.

P.S. It's about ten and I'm back from church and just had supper. . . . I'm glad I went to Dr Hutton; he was at the far side of London. His text was: 'We know not whither we are going. . . . "I am the way".' He began about Christ's promise of a spiritual presence. How much of our thinking is really about material things? Man after man in the street, but the mind behind the face is working over again that quarrel with a friend yesterday, that broken hope, that undeserved failure. Speak to him, and he'll answer with cheerfulness and gusto – the heroic convention that hides a troubled spirit. But we live with ghosts. . . . Christ never answered a question. He knew no answer is of any use to us except what we find for ourselves. Oh Peggy, it's true. And all the way to church I'd been fighting down that dull despondency, partly because I'd been looking at the flaming Christmas book lists and wishing the *Scholars* had been there; thinking that it would come out unnoticed at Easter, and likely too late for a decent job, and I'd go on in the wilderness till I was too old to be anything but a hack. . . . All because of eight wasted years doing my duty as I saw it. . . . But tonight has shut me up I hope for life. 'Never ask questions about the Absolute. The Absolute becomes relative when it touches you.' It has linked up in my head with that picture in Ben Hur, the cross swaying above the heads of the crowd. Not that anything we've ever done is worth anything. But that shuts your mouth.

I must stop and go to bed. It comforts me to find that Dr Hutton sits and mourns over his 'unmerited misfortunes'!

Next day: I'm getting on with the first draft. I just can't tell you the relief of finding it's really working out. I get so frightened and depressed, and all my notes seem so poor and meagre and dull. Then a fresh morning comes and I'm swimming before I know. But it's a dog's life too! However,

Leonard Atkinson has asked me to go with him to a dinner in aid of some Fund at the Savoy. The Prince of Wales is to be the guest of honour. It's tomorrow, and I'm awfully feared that I'll have to get a pukha evening dress. I said I'd go before I remembered how very afternoonish my dresses are. Of course I knew I'd have to get one sometime, but I'm depressed. . . . It is a queer world. It's such a waste! There's three men all wasted. And me that could have loved terribly, and was born to have a house and children and a man, solitary up four flights of stairs writing a book! I've been working hard and am a bit tired. It will get finished all right, but sometimes it seems like climbing Donard – hill on top of hill.

CHAPTER VIII

The Wandering Scholars *and* Medieval Latin Lyrics

Helen's long association with the publishing firm of Constable had begun even before she left Belfast. In 1915 they had published her *Lyrics from the Chinese*, and when she came to London she met the various partners of the firm in person. Her first meeting with the senior partner, Mr Otto Kyllmann, was important, and very soon her friendship was consolidated with the other partners, who included Mr Alan Agnew, Mr Michael Sadler and Miss Margaret (Martha) Smith.

Throughout the intermediate period between writing as a freelance and her acceptance of a permanent post, she also continued to correct vast quantities of examination papers, and in fact, became a chief examiner. This trait of persistence in her make-up is a rather surprising contrast to her habitual emotional motivation of thought and action.

Years of research in the British Museum in London and in the *Bibliothèque Nationale* in Paris, preceded the writing of *The Wandering Scholars*. Her letters after 1925 described the gestation period, the final birth and the breathtaking success of the book itself.

In 1926 when Helen had fixed an appointment with Mr Kyllmann, whose courtesy was as instinctive as his perceptive judgement of authors and the works brought to him: and, in this case, his susceptibility to attractive women had been roused in an earlier encounter with Helen, so this meeting was eminently successful for both parties, and Meg gets an ecstatic letter:

Mr. Kyllmann was utterly benevolent: he wants the book –

wants a *big* book, and has given me *carte blanche* to say everything I want, appendices and all the rest of it. And he is already talking about a simultaneous American edition, and getting it read by Edmund Gosse. He says it's madness for me to attempt it by July. Let him have it in October, to come out in the New Year – thinks it much the best time and that you get more attention in the early spring for a book of this kind. I think he is right. He's elderly, Constable's director, very sardonic and engaging, and delightful manners. We get on well – you know I *do* get on with that type. And he takes my kind of joke. And he *does* want my book. I can't believe it's me, Peggy. To have a publisher taking it for granted that you'll be worth 'the full column in *The Sunday Times*' as he said casually. Well, the agony and the sweat begin again tomorrow, but I have had my day.

The beginning that you saw is scrapped, and several more, but today's I think good – so does Professor Spurgeon. The solid ground is at last under my feet. And it makes all the difference in the world to have certainty before me. (Of course we didn't discuss terms: contracts will come later.) But I am safe.

And darling, Saintsbury has offered to read my proofs!

In the early months of 1927 the book was completed, and Helen could announce the glad tidings to Meg:

I've written to Kyllmann to find out if he can give me till, say, the third week in March. I've sent off the first 90 pages of the last revise, and they are now beginning to print it off. Odd the sense of finality it leaves one with. . . . You can't touch it any more. Did you see Saintsbury's review in *The Observer*? Several people have asked me about it since. There'll be a new batch of proofs today. They look beautiful, and the prospectus, of which I've just corrected the proofs, is very agreeable.

I could go on writing to you for ever. I sleep so much better when you are here. But I've no fault with life just now – the work is so good. I always wanted to be finishing the book in spring, and there's a blackbird or a thrush out in the trees on Primrose Hill, that's just beginning – half a dozen pipes, over and over. And it's a rainy twilight, like so many twilights in February that I remember at that bedroom window in Cedar Avenue, with only wet roofs and redbrick chimneys, but somewhere a blackbird calling, and my heart nearly breaking for life and the promise of adventure. And now I'm nearing it, in my own flat in London, with a book nearly written, and so much good life behind me, and maybe better still in front. But I was a good dreamer, even then.

Do you remember Columbanus? 'Yet what is life but a road? And none of them who walk upon it make their dwelling in the road, for they have their dwelling in their own country.' Must stop and return to the Xth century – it should be finished tonight.

And then a few weeks later: 'They showed me the *Scholars* on Saturday in the office, not yet released and no paper jacket, but I think you'll burst with pride. It's far beyond my dreams, and the illustrations are lovely.'

In April 1927, *The Wandering Scholars* was released to the public. A spate of eulogistic reviews followed, and Helen shared her gratification with Meg as soon as the book reached Kilmacrew:

I was overjoyed to get your letter. I am thinking about you continually. Och, my wee Bun, I do so want to see you. And what a love you are to hop so about the book. . . . I am sending the *Glasgow Herald* review, also a very scholarly whole full column in *The Times Educational Supplement* – 'This is an outstanding book.' The *Litt. Supp.* hasn't spoken yet. But there's one just out in *The Saturday Review*, awfully enthusiastic, a full column: 'Not even lavish quotation and profuse illustration can do justice to Miss Waddell's graceful, accomplished and scholarly essay in medieval literature.'

Very soon *The Times* (not the *Literary Supplement* but the ordinary one) published a review: 'that pleased me for *The Times* itself doesn't often review unless rather important things. . . . I liked "the mind of a scholar and the pen of a wit".'

Of the reviewer in *The Manchester Guardian* Helen wrote: 'He's the only man who has seen what I was really driving at – "the secret struggle and ardours of these vanished scholars", and he adds: "I doubt if she realises what an amazing achievement the book is – lovely and considered prose." '

Professor Saintsbury's review in *The Observer* brought her congratulations, and offers from publishers and editors for whatever she wrote in the future. And Walter de La Mare wrote to O.K.* about the book: 'She writes about poetry absolutely unknown to me, in a fashion that is itself poetry.'

But a letter from O.K. which she found waiting for her after a return from Kilmacrew, pleased her more than anything.

May 1927

> I am not sure when you will be back, but I want to send you a line before your book is publicly acclaimed. . . . I am of course quite unable to express an opinion to which you will attach any value, but for my own satisfaction I want to tell you how much I admire your work. Some of your translations are in my opinion exquisite. Then again you have a beautiful gift of words. You create an interest in the men of whom you write. I am no scholar and I take off my hat to your scholarship, but I stand covered and salute your power to weave a spell. Forgive this ill-expressed screed, but perhaps you will understand that it is your love of humanity and your charity that shine through the beautifully chosen words.
>
> O.K.

Success such as this did not change Helen's personality, but it certainly changed her outlook on daily life. Freedom from fear of the future vanished: uncongenial jobs faded from her mind. Research and advice for Constable's was entirely to her taste as

*O.K., Otto Kyllmann.

a scholar, as well as a basic safeguard against financial shortages. She was free to give rein to poetry and prose, translations, lectures, reviews, books – anything that would satisfy her creative spirit and her genius for words.

'Life is so exciting,' she wrote to Meg.

> 'I can hardly bear it, and tonight I am just dying for Killy and the soft voices of the ducks in the bog, wicked as they are. . . . The English tutor at Westfield, who always liked me, wrote that she was "intoxicated" with *The Scholars*. . . . Isn't it a mercy I didn't get a job there?'
>
> Your letter only just in, and I am happy. Couldn't quite settle down till you had pranced. . . . Darling, did I tell you I was among the best-sellers last week? It is such a funny grudging notice in *The Observer*. I think all publishers send in their figures once a week, and the other books have been out for weeks and well reviewed: mine was out ten days and yet second in the list – and this before Saintsbury's review. Constable's window is full of nothing else. Just seven copies in a row.

Inevitably Helen had numerous publishers offering her work: O.K. chuckled and said, 'I told you so! This is the first, but it won't be the last, my dear. They'll all be after you!' And indeed they were.

The book had paid for itself in two months from publication and O.K. was thinking of a third edition. The American edition came out before the end of May and had as great a réclame as the one in England. Helen told Meg that 'everyone in Constable's treats me as if I were the Queen of Sheba'.

It would be impossible to exaggerate the success of *The Wandering Scholars*, but space is too limited to include more than a few of the reactions that Helen repeated to her sister.

One came from Naomi Mitchison:

> I have just finished reading *The Wandering Scholars*. It is a book one can linger over as indefinitely as on a hillside of flowers,

and my husband and I have been browsing for months. Now I want to say thank you. It is all five centuries later than any time in history I have dealt with, fifteen centuries later than the time I am happiest in. I had thought of it, as most people I suppose do, as the Dark Ages, hopelessly marred by one's lesson-book wars and rebellions. I had known some of the later Latin hymns, but had no idea of the wealth of material and all these light and violent things you have set out for us. It has made that time properly alive for me, and must have for a good many others, for I think one need not be a scholar to appreciate either your book or its matter – though doubtless I have missed many of its best points, and sometimes been so breathlessly carried away on your leaping sentences.

I should very much like to meet you. . . . I wonder if you know Eileen Power; she is a very great friend of mine. Could we manage some joint meal in London, and I could ask you questions?

Yours sincerely,

NAOMI MITCHISON

Soon after Helen records a meeting:

Very full of work, getting ahead with the Lyrics. Eileen Power told us that Arnold Bennett met her at a dinner-party and talked about nothing but *The Wandering Scholars* all the evening. . . . It was a good party at the Mitchisons. Julian Huxley was there. And on Tuesday I lunch with American publisher, and that evening hear Suggia play at the Hudson's. . . .

The Gobi Three start for China again in about two weeks. . . . They're going to keep a diary this time, and will send it to me to prepare for publication. They are so good and so merry it makes you feel that they've found the only way to live. They had a sister, a Mrs. Murray Robertson from Dublin, a sardonic, amazingly intelligent woman, quoting Baudelaire and Proust. She says our brother Sam, is the greatest actor she has ever seen. Dublin goes wild over him, and that he is a terrible loss to the professional stage.

The Royal Society of Literature asked Helen if she would accept a medal for *The Wandering Scholars* in the A. C. Benson Foundation:

'I haven't a notion what it's all about but I'll ask O.K., and meantime I'm frightfully bucked.'

And a week later she writes:

> Lady Rhondha has asked me to dinner. . . . And darling, I'm beginning to think more of the Royal Society medal for people are so fussed about it. They don't give it very often it seems. They have given *gold* medals three times – Sir Walter Scott, and Meredith and Kipling. And the silver medal to D'Annunzio and Barrie, and Galdos and Santanyana, and Gordon Bottomley and Lytton Strachey. But I'm the only woman. . . . Their secretary told O.K. that the Selection Committee were wild about the book. I wrote to L.M.H. and Miss Grier is simply drunk. So is Professor Spurgeon. . . . Darling, I can't believe it's true about the medal, can you?

Then came the presentation at an afternoon tea-party, for which she tells Meg: 'I must be very elegant'; and when it was over:

> Yesterday was really a success. Dean Inge who made the presentation was just a dear with such a sad face. He said the book had made a 'positive sensation', and spoke about its mixture of learning and charm. . . . And afterwards Sir Henry Newbolt, the President of the Society, told me the judging committee were all extremely distinguished, and *every one* had sent in my name with specially hearty recommendations. . . . And the medal is really lovely.

In the autumn of 1928, Helen was invited by the Council to

be elected to the Fellowship of the Royal Society of Literature, and she naturally accepted.

A year earlier she had written a paper on 'John of Salisbury' (Thomas à Becket's secretary) for the English Association. It was acclaimed and published in their annual collection of 'Essays and Studies'. By 1939 she had developed a full length biography of John of Salisbury, but publication was deferred by the outbreak of war. The material remains scattered among her hand-written papers, and it is possible that enough has been rescued for eventual publication.

One more letter has been selected for the interest of its source:

To Meg:

. . . Was enormously cheered by a letter from the Abbé Brémond* – an extraordinarily witty and brilliant French Scholar, rather like Anatole France. I'd been in correspondence with him about a book for Constable, and finally sent him *The Wandering Scholars*.

He writes: 'Your book has been a sheer delight to me. You will find me *très vaniteux*, but reading it I said to myself at almost every page "*Mais est-ce bien elle, n'est-ce plutôt moi qui ai écrit ce livre?*" (But is it really she, is it not I who wrote this book?) Apart from the marvellous translations, there is a note *très français* and – bear with me – Brémondicum? God knows that I adore English scholarship, but here there is a *je ne sais quoi* beyond it, that enchants me.'

When the spate of letters about *The Wandering Scholars* died down, Helen began serious work on selection and translation of the lyrics of her 'vagantes', and Constable's published them

*Brémond, L'Abbé Henri (1865–1933), historian and critic, withdrew from the Jesuit Order and from teaching in Jesuit schools to devote himself to writing and research. He spent several years in religious establishments in England and Wales. His chief work was *Histoire littéraire de sentiment religieux en France* (1916–33, 11 vols), a study of the religious element in French literature from the end of the Wars of Religion (1562–96), and particularly of the part played by mysticism.

under the title *Medieval Latin Lyrics*, in the autumn of 1929. The reviews were favourable and her success was almost complete. Helen sent Meg delighted letters and quotes from two reviews that she especially liked:

> Two years ago Miss Waddell produced in *The Wandering Scholars* one of those very rare books which are at once pioneer work and virtually final. To that most remarkable book she has now provided a supplement, fully worthy of her critical history. It is both a document and a delight. Miss Waddell must henceforth have place with the first of our translators from Frere, Henry Francis Cary, to Dante Gabriel Rossetti and Arthur Symons.

And another:

> Miss Waddell has kept her promise well: she promised a volume of translations from the lyrics of those fascinating 'vagantes'. Some indeed are among the loveliest in any literature; and Miss Waddell has not dulled their brightness. She has come to them not merely with scholarship and literary tact, but with a soul attuned to the thought and feeling and the very idiom of another day. She has the most important of all the translator's qualifications – a perfect sympathy with her material. '*Hora dat feminiam*'.

To balance the picture, unfavourable criticism must not be ignored, although this would be negligible if it had not included the name of the famous medievalist, George Gordon Coulton, lecturer in English and Fellow of St John's College, Cambridge, author of a giant series of Medieval Studies which made him an international expert and acknowledged authority on the Middle Ages.

Helen discussed him with Meg:

> Did you see G. G. Coulton's whack at me in last week's *Observer*? Don't know why the old boy hates me so, unless because he was at the Middle Ages long before me, and also

that he is an almost venomous Protestant. Saintsbury is neither to hold nor to bind – calls him 'the immeasurable ass', and says I satisfied the most austere critic in England, Sir Frederick Pollock, etc. etc. I've written a very brief and really funny letter to the *Observer*, not as much poking fun at Coulton as at P. S. Allen in Chicago who said I 'fuzzed the Middle Ages' in his book, and who lately dismissed the researches of his more distinguished fellow medievalists, Wiener, Faral and Winterfeld, as 'the running about of persons who have published so pretentiously in the field of my effort'.

A year later G. G. Coulton challenged four more points, one a genuine misprint.

He apologised for troubling me, but 'it was all in the interests of exact scholarship'. I again replied temperately and gratefully, and 'in return' as I said, pointed out a howler in his own last book in which he mistook St. Hugh of Cluny for a very inferior abbot, Hugh of Flavigny, and on that based an indictment of all momentum in the eleventh century. I did not describe it as a howler, only stated the facts, with reference to original sources which Coulton had not used. I think it gave him the shock of his life. However, he controlled himself, thanked me politely, and with considerably more respect than before explained naively that he had been having a controversy with a friend of his, a scholar of great eminence, as to whether my book had any value as a 'contribution to knowledge' apart from its 'exceptional literary excellence'. He enclosed a 'charge sheet' in which he brought about a dozen charges against the book, and wound up with a few vicious sneers about window-dressing and so on. This he said, he had sent on to my champion some time ago. Again I controlled my temper (for after all he is an old man, fantastically Protestant and a savage controversialist. One Catholic scholar said of him: 'the law of correspondence with Dr. Coulton is the survival of the rudest'), and I replied quietly as a summer day. 'I am on your side in this controversy, with reservations. I am no scholar: but I am tolerably industrious, and I hope, a tolerably honest student of the Middle Ages. *The Wandering Scholars* was a first book, written with all the passion and most of the faults of an amateur, except one: respect for evidence, and preference for primary authorities: it was further marred by the fact that I am, I think, the worst proof-reader in the world. I could supply you from my marginal notes and corrections for the last five years with ammunition far more deadly than you have here.' I then handled his charges, blandly indicating the opinions of Haskins (the chief expert in America), Powicke (for England) and Ferdinand Lot (for France) on *The Wandering Scholars*, and bowed myself out. The result has been incredible: on the points at issue he will probably wrangle as long as he lives, but as to the book as a whole he has just collapsed, and in such a decent letter. It must have cost him agony to write it. 'It is hard even for an old man, and one nearing the end of his work, not to feel jealous. . . . And I had been challenged to say the worst I knew. . . . I had my back to the wall. It was my own reputation that was challenged.' I could have wept when I read that letter. So I wrote him, almost affectionately, asking his forgiveness if in any way I had seemed impertinent to a 'man of his vast erudition'. So the end is peace. But it has really been rather dreadful, for he is a kind of Mussalman in a holy war. I think it was worth doing, for he was a deadly reviewer. 'Just hint a sneer and hesitate dislike' is his method, when he isn't downright savage.

Bless you, my darling. Such a waste of time. And yet really it removes a kind of poison spring – and in Cambridge of all places. I have no idea who my unknown champion was.

CHAPTER IX

The Fruitful Years

After the success of the *Medieval Latin Lyrics* Helen tried to concentrate on *Peter Abelard*, the novel that had been in her mind since her schooldays in Belfast. How she achieved the seemingly impossible is the thread that runs through her life and work from 1929 to 1933, when the result finally appeared.

Fame came to her as scholar and authoress, as poet and lecturer, as witty speaker with a supremely beautiful voice and a magnetic personality, all of which attracted an attention which is overwhelming in retrospect. Her sister Meg remained her *alter ego* and outlet, and Kilmacrew her heart's home. Fundamental humility ruled her attitude to the heights and depths of her conscious emotions and the years she lived by herself in her own little flat held tranquillity and produced the high spots of her creative genius.

Yet it was from Ormonde Terrace that she made her sorties into the social world of friendly celebrities who were holding out their hands to her. Naively she passed on her reactions to Meg, but her head was never turned in conceit. Her humility took the danger out of flattery; her sense of humour was as fundamental as her instinct to sublimate platonic love, and her own virginity which she retained throughout her life. In the quiet of her flat by herself, she found refreshment and repose, freedom from the demands of other people on her time and on her compassion.

From her letters at this period it is obvious that she appreciated most the praise of scholars and serious authors, headed, of course, by Professors Saintsbury and Gregory Smith; followed in second place by Sir Frederick Pollock (Professor of Common Law, Inns of Court and a Privy Councillor); J. W. Mackail (President of the Classical Association); and Gilbert Murray (Regius Professor of Greek at Oxford). Among her literary friends and admirers were poets and writers, some English or Scottish, some from Ireland: 'A.E.', W. B. Yeats, Stephen Gwynn, John Buchan, Rose Macaulay, Virginia Woolf, Enid Starkie, John Sparrow, Charles Morgan, George Buchanan and many others. Chance threw her into contact with several art collectors, elderly men such as 'Mr Hudson' with his 'lovely house in Queen Anne's Gate', where she met the Portuguese cellist Suggia, and the Aranyi sisters, both violinists; also Sir Robert Witt, the well-known collector of photographed prints, who formed a library of pictures and drawings from all schools of art in his Portland Square house and opened it to serious students.

Several men in diplomatic or political posts became Helen's great friends, all being attracted in the first place by her Latin translations and most having aspirations in the same field. Notable among them was Sir Basil Blackett, who had recently returned from India after six years as Finance Member of the Executive Council under two Viceroys, Lord Reading and Lord Halifax. He introduced Stanley Baldwin to her at the former's request. And Helen met Baron Palmstierna, the Swedish Minister to the Court of St James, at his house, and in all probability many others of the political names mentioned casually in her letters.

She was always very faithful to friends from her home and youth in Ireland, and membership of the Irish Society of Literature was a strong link between them all. But the friendship with Otto Kyllmann ('O.K.'), begun during the publication of *The Wandering Scholars*, gradually became the pivot of both their lives: even the gulf of twenty years in age and absence of beard was overcome. Helen's deepest compassion was roused by the loneliness of a still attractive man who had experienced two broken marriages and had an invalid daughter. No doubt their friendship deepened as they walked on the Wiltshire Downs on Sunday afternoons. A poem that Helen wrote and sent to Basil Blackett (among other friends) must have been inspired by its title – '*Martinsell*'.

The Sun shone out on Martinsell.
  And warmed the barrows of the dead.
The Down was topaz at our feet,
  And the sky sapphire that was lead.

And love that had been in our hearts,
  Long suffering and grave and dumb,
Leapt to his stature, with a light
  Disdained the shining of the sun.

The sun went in behind a cloud.
  The barrows of the dead were cold.
More ancient they than their high trees,
  This stone beside them not more old.

And is our passion brief as light?
  Shall nothing but the dead abide?
Still in their barrows, and outlive
  The ecstasy they knew and died?

Or is their passion in this place
  As present as their ancient peace,
But only those that are their peers
  In love, can give that love release?

The dead are dead: their ecstasy
  Eternity itself doth own.
This moment of this day outlasts
  Even this imperishable stone.

Helen's days were occupied with important advisory work for Constable's and with new ideas and interesting suggestions. Interspersed were lectures, reviews and translations, but somehow she managed to transfer her own creative writing to paper too.

She also persisted in fairly frequent brief visits to Kilmacrew, and was lionised in Belfast and Dublin, to the pride and joy of her relatives and family. She became known as 'Ulster's darling', and Queen's University spoke of her as 'the most distinguished woman of her generation' (which Helen dismissed as 'by way of civility to Queen's of course, but very gratifying').

When one particular visit to Kilmacrew was over she wrote to Meg on her way back to London:

> It nearly broke my heart leaving you yesterday, but there's no good talking. It seems harder every time. . . . I think Kilmacrew is the kindest house I know, and the most human – a kind of hearth of the world, and turf burning there. Maude said long ago that it was full of you, and very like you, and if that was true ten years ago the flavour has deepened so. You don't know what a rare person you are.

Nearly every letter that follows begins with much the same opening: 'Working hard and full of new ideas for the firm. O.K. frightfully pleased. . . . The latest thing I want them to do is to print *Coleridge's Notebook* with the "Ancient Mariner" stuff in it; it's in the British Museum. Going down now to look at it.'

Or she gives Meg a list of the work to be done:

> I am now gathering courage to (1) write a brief introduction to Charlotte Clarke (funny 18th-century autobiography I came on); (2) to write to Thornton Wilder to suggest that he write a life of Keats (he is oddly like Keats himself); (3) to write to Walter Starkie in Dublin to suggest a book on the influence of Spain on English Literature; (4) to write to Enid Starkie who asked me for advice about the construction of her book on Baudelaire; (5) to report on a MS on Charles I and his first Parliament; (6) to report on A. P. Grave's MS of Irish poems; (7) to write to Lowe about the Coleridge Notebook; (8) to write to Sir Michael Sadler about his collection; (9) to finish a review on Villon for the *New Adelphi*, Middleton Murry's quarterly, which should have been done for the Christmas number, alas.

Then she breaks off and recounts her outside social activities:

Yesterday I had lunch with Mr. Hudson at Queen Anne's Gate; four of us, J. B. Trend who is Spanish adviser to Constable, and a wonderful old Spanish Marquis, enormously interested in my conviction that Spain is coming to its own in literature again, and all of them very flattering about my books. . . . And I'm dining at Mr. Hudson's next Wednesday. Darling, it's all so dreadful that I shall sit over the fire and do nothing. May McKisack and her mother were here last night, and I've suggested to May that she do the Life and Letters of Sir Thomas More, and she is on her knees to me for the sheer beauty of it, her present work being Parliamentary Boroughs in the 14th century. . . . And, darling, though I haven't written I've been in a turmoil of things. I was dining with the Ellis Roberts, and Jack was here when they brought me home. And Ellis said: 'That nephew of yours is all the Kipling novels in one, exactly the type'! Next day I went down to lunch with Viola Garvin and Humbert Wolfe, and then had to see Harris the new editor of the *Nineteenth Century and After*. He asked me to get the 'Ministry of All Talents' together. So I've already bagged Humbert Wolfe and Saintsbury.

. . . This was my last week's dossier, besides a lot of smaller stuff, such as revising Saintsbury's proof corrections, which no one but me can read. And then there was a dinner with Gustav Holst and Clifford Bax, both dears about comic opera, which is now written as far as words go, only I have to help with bits of it. And tomorrow Mr. Hudson takes me in his car to his Jacobean house in Sussex, along with Suggia.

Then a postscript is added:

The British Broadcasting people want me 'to give a series on medieval things – come to lunch with the Director of Talks and discuss it'. Oh darling, it's very flattering, but I don't want to – not this winter. If I don't get at my novel I don't know what will happen to me, and it's always one thing more between me and it. And things like the B.B.C. and lecturing turn my knees to water beforehand. I'll talk to O.K. and

Michael Sadler about it anyhow, but I thought you would be pleased. O.K. says it never does any harm to be hard to get hold of.

Helen must have worked on several books concurrently: perhaps the effort was facilitated by her customary routine of going down to Constable's offices in the mornings, and returning to Ormonde Terrace to more writing and social gaieties in the afternoons and evenings. She was stimulated by each success, yet all her life she refused to lower the standards she set herself. However the imagination and emotional participation her novel, the immortal story of Abelard and Héloise, could only be brought to birth in the repose and solitude of her own flat. As she tells Meg: 'The Abelard chapters are pretty good, I think, but upon my word they nearly kill me, for you live the things while you're writing them.' But she could translate, despatch business or private correspondence, and edit, or correct, in the intervals between consultations at the office, and she did so with consistent effect.

A cutting from *Punch* in June 1931 sums up the situation:

Miss Helen Waddell strikes me as in danger of earning, here and now, a pre-mortuary epitaph: the '*Nullum quod tetigit non ornavit*' (he touched nothing that he did not adorn) that Dr. Johnson transferred from Fénelon's *Cicero* to his own *Oliver Goldsmith*. First it was *The Wandering Scholars*, then *Medieval Latin Lyrics*, then the memorable preface to *Cole's Paris Journal*; and now an excellent translation of *The History of the Chevalier Des Grieux and of Manon Lescaut* . . . in which it shows that leisure can still be found for an unassuming classic to be rendered to perfection. She has been able to retain much of the rhythm of the Abbé Prévost's masterpiece in a narrative that reads as racily as *The Vicar of Wakefield*.

Professor Saintsbury wrote the Introduction, and Helen used the story later on as the basis of a play.

In the same year of 1931 Constable published a selection of

Latin short stories and verse, entitled *A Book of Medieval Latin for Schools*. Helen's reactions to the labour of writing it were, as usual, passed on to Meg: 'The little Reader is driving me frantic – or would, only for Marjorie Broughall at Norwich who is doing the vocabulary, and is such an absolute brick and so fond of me. You know, darling, we do like people who love us, because they enjoy us.'

Helen, in her introduction explains her purpose: 'This book is frankly an experiment: that it is being tried at all is due to the determination of the Classical Panel of the Association of Assistant Mistresses, and especially of its Convenor, (Miss Marjorie Broughall), whom I have to thank for a tireless expense of time and trouble, and for taking on herself the whole burden of the vocabulary.'

The success of the experiment is conclusively proved by Constable's having reprinted ten editions of it between 1931 and 1962; and it is still selling well. Even that awe-inspiring scholar G. G. Coulton reviewed it favourably, saying: 'The editor's name is a warrant for the literary excellence of this book . . . not only as a manual that may add to the gaiety and vitality of school reading, but it is also a booklet which a scholar might well slip into his rucksack for his holiday.'

Helen accomplished a third piece of work in the same year and tells Meg about it:

> I have been devilling hard at that review for the *Scottish Historical* and just got it sent off, and then I had the great excitement of a new discovery in the M.S. room at the British Museum – an old diary, 1766–1770, kept by an old antiquarian parson (the Rev. William Cole), who was an intimate friend of Horace Walpole and knew Gray. . . . There's also a three month diary about a visit to Paris with Walpole. Went nearly drunk, and half-way through rang up O.K. and went to the office. Michael Sadleir came down: all worries fell from him and he said: 'Let's telephone to have it copied at once. Will anybody get it while you're sitting here?' You can imagine they're pleased down at the office. I'd love to have

copied it myself, but they said it would be a waste of my time. But oh so restful! He's so like the Boss (Meg's husband). Mr. Stanzer came to see me at 10, and nearly stunned me with talking.

The reviews when the book came out were all favourable. One from Virginia Woolf pleased Helen so much that she asks Meg: 'Don't you love Virginia Woolf – "A purr of content and anticipation rose from half the armchairs in England"?' (This review was written in the form of a long letter to Helen and printed later in one of Virginia's own books, *Death of the Moth*.)

In the following year (1932) Helen began to work more regularly on her novel, but after writing two chapters in a week:

. . . the first act of a play to be called *The Abbé Prévost* blazed into my head. It's based on the story of his life. . . . I see the whole thing. *How* I wish I could read it to you, but maybe I'll have it all finished in a week or two. Darling, do forgive this crazy ramble, but I'm full of it. I'm to dine tonight to meet Max Beerbohm again. Saturday is the Baldwin lunch, and today I'm lunching with Professor Lowes.

She took the half-finished play to Kilmacrew and showed it to her brother, Sam, and to Lennox Robinson, both of them actors and playwrights connected with the Abbey Theatre in Dublin. Helen read the play to them, and

the minute I had finished Lennox flung himself into discussing how to produce it on the stage, tons of theatrical advice and so on, but said really nothing as to whether he thought it good or not, except that he begged me not to let anyone inferior have it. . . . I wasn't exactly dashed, but just interested and indifferent. . . . They said once *what* a chance it gave good actors, so I suppose they liked it, and somehow I have a queer belief in the thing myself.

Shortly after Helen returned to London from Ireland the play 'blazed' still more strongly in her mind and a letter immediately went to Meg:

Darling,

Am almost dizzy with excitement. O.K. was seeing the Shaws yesterday at their flat, and asked him for advice about where to send the play, and he got frightfully interested – and then the dear old lady came in (I call her dear for reasons soon to be obvious) and sat down a little tired after her first walk out since she broke her arm, and said: 'Who wrote it?' And O.K. said: 'A friend of mine, Helen Waddell', and she shot up and said: 'Who wrote those two beautiful books?' And then went on in great fuss and buzz, about the lyrics and the beauty of the books – and then said: 'Is *he* going to read the play?' 'I never dreamt of asking that,' says O.K., 'I was just asking advice.' 'Of course I'll read it,' says G.B.S. 'We'll both read it – and if I think I can do anything with it, I'll take it to Barry Jackson* or Leon Lion† myself.' Darling, think of having G.B.S. as one's dramatic agent!!

Of course it mayn't come to much – you know when one is very old, one forgets easily, and G.B.S. *is* very old now, though Rosamond saw him tearing along Kingsway the other night in bitter frost with no overcoat, tall and thin, and walking like a windmill. But isn't it just amazing – and that good old Charlotte Shaw should have read the books?

Postscript. I've just turned back and put the *Care*! at the beginning, because the merest scrap of publicity about Shaw is worth anything to the papers, and it might just spoil everything. I mean, suppose the Boss told Mr. Lusk and it got into the *Chronicle*, then it's the *Whig*, and then the fat's in the fire. I'm very bitter at the moment, for someone got hold of the Baldwin lunch, and three papers, Bristol and Newcastle and the *Weekly Dispatch* from Manchester have kicked off with 'Mr. Baldwin, who made the fortune of Mary Webb, is now

*Producer.

†Actor-manager.

interested in another woman writer', and so on. I think I know who did it, a woman who was at lunch with Mr. Ellis (the Superintendent of the Reading Room) and me, about a fortnight ago, and whom I don't trust the length of a door-scraper, but I had no idea she had any connection with the press, just thought she haunted the Museum and gossiped there. I can hardly look at her now, for she even told *how* the lunch came about, and describes me as 'a lively little Irish woman, with a thick brogue and an impish wit' – all frightfully intimate. As Maude says, that will anyhow keep Baldwin from thinking it's myself who wrote it! I'll see if I can find the damnable object, but I think I threw them all three in the fire.

So don't tell even the Boss just yet. He is so happy and so dreadfully indiscreet. I feel that if Baldwin ever reads his press cuttings, it's enough to make him eschew my name for life. And you don't know the tiny trifles that make a paragraph about Shaw. This would be like News from the Front compared to most of them. 'G.B.S. turns Dramatic Agent'. 'G.B.S. and the Wandering Scholar'. 'Charlotte and G.B.S. read a Play'.

But oh my love, if it comes to anything – Shaw says it ought to be 'set up', i.e. roughly printed to give it a really good chance, the way he does his own, and O.K. says he is going to print me about 35 copies privately for a Christmas present. Isn't it wonderful?

And then, after a short wait:

G.B.S. has read the play, but only spoke on the telephone. He was down in the country and phoning about something else, but interrupted himself with: 'About your young friend's play, it ought to do. A charming action for Lenki, and she's got Prévost, but the difficulty will be to get an actor good enough for the part. But I'll write you about it. That's the worst I can say of it!'

I'm terribly bucked, for I was afraid he'd pooh-pooh it

altogether. But still keep it dark. I am hoping for his letter to O.K., but the old man is frightfully busy with his Shaw–Ellen Terry letters.

Bernard Shaw, as Helen feared, did forget. Nothing more is heard of the play until the spring of 1935.

CHAPTER X

Incidental Activities and Work

Helen's life might have become a social whirl, but as long as she lived in Ormonde Terrace, without domestic chores, she managed to dedicate a fair proportion of her evenings to her own creative writing.

Slowly her novel *Peter Abelard* took shape, and Meg followed its progress chapter by chapter.

Of course there were interruptions, big and small. A significant one came from the University of Durham, which offered Helen the honorary degree of D.Litt. It was significant in that it was the first of several that other universities in Great Britain and the United States gave her in later years. A somewhat disjointed letter to Meg, written in the train taking her back to London, describes the occasion:

> I don't know where to begin. It was a most awful strain, hour after hour, but one of the great moments in one's life. A cathedral like Chartres, and oneself part of the great procession – choir, cross, Bishop of Durham. Londonderry superb in his robes, and then the new doctors, two by two, blazing in scarlet – and convocation – I the only woman in a long long line of men, and almost stamping with excitement, and the magic of great shows. And then passing up into the choir, and the double column separating before the altar and climbing to the carved canons' seats – I beside Eddington. And then the Te Deum, and the Bishop's sermon, and Londonderry sitting rather like a Byzantine mosaic, and then the recessional to the Chapterhouse for the degrees. It began at eleven when I, solitary, was taken to the great tapestried room

in the Castle to robe. Londonderry and Lord Dawson of Penn and all the great ones, but all men and no looking glass, robes scarlet with gold borders, and gorgeous gold hood – black velvet cap like the Oxford ones. Livingstone charming to me, and the Bishop of Gloucester – and Londonderry on whose right I sat at lunch – well, if he wasn't a practised old hand at the job, I would be preening myself on my unusual graces. Seriously, he insisted over and over that I was to come and stay – that I was to let them know when I came to you, and stay at Mountstewart. I said goodbye to him at the garden party and he again urged: 'You promise to come?' Also Lord Dawson of Penn and I almost parted embracing.

But oh the panic! We were all robed and waiting, waiting, waiting. Heard the chant outside – for they install the Chancellor in the Castle Courtyard on the steps. Then comes the Vice-Chancellor, my host, and the Proctors, to fetch the Chancellor-elect, and the procession forms. Londonderry with his Highland pipers – sheer pomp and splendour. I've seen nothing like it, and the cathedral service gave it just the medieval solemnity. I'm dying to see you and tell you all about it.

Rose Macaulay comes into the picture too, after Helen had advised Meg to read *They were Defeated*:

It's seventeenth century and a story almost like Abelard and Héloise. I was so moved by it that I sat down and wrote her a letter, which I repented afterwards for she is a very caustic, critical creature. But she wrote to me: 'That you should feel it real, or good in any way, is the nicest thing, almost, that could happen to it. And, above all, that you should feel as you do about Julian's story and end, which were very near my own heart. I feared her death might be too facile an escape and solution, but it seemed inevitable, and that she had already died, and that the blow which killed, therefore, wasn't a bolt from the blue. I don't know though. Anyhow you like the book, and I am so proud that you do! I did love doing it, but have made so many mistakes. . . . I do hope we may meet, and talk of these things sometime. I hear you are writing of Abelard: how splendid that will be.'

Diplomats and politicians mingle with poets and authors frequently as, for instance, Walter de la Mare and Stanley Baldwin, and Helen tells Meg:

I am to lunch with Basil Blackett some Saturday and meet Mr. Baldwin by special request of the same. Sir Basil and he were at the same house-party last week, and got talking about my books, and Baldwin said he had been wanting to meet me for years, so Basil said he would try to arrange it with me. Darling, isn't it fun? Let us hold hands and say 'Hee-Haw!'.

After the meeting Helen writes:

I just fell for Baldwin. Not a bit like his stockbroker's photographs, but rather like a classical scholar turned farmer, with a kind of innocence about him. I was beside him at lunch and we talked hard, but most of all about the Wiltshire downs. He made his last cabinet in a funny little village called Oare, just two miles from Pewsey where you and I were. He was extravagant in praise of *The Scholars*, said I'd put him forever in my debt; the *Lyrics* likewise.

The poet appears on another occasion:

Met de la Mare again and Lady Oxford – you know, Margot Asquith, nutcracker face, smouldering dark eyes, but such fun – a kind of reckless tongue and a terrible egoist, but really almost irresistible. She is so alive and so impish. . . . This is a stupid letter, but it took me a long time to recover from Margot. I think she drains you rather. De la Mare crept over to me after it, and sat beside me like a mouse, and said: 'Can you really do with this kind of talk?' And we held hands spiritually and said how nice it was to be slow and stupid, and we talked infantine uneconomic things, and I am to meet him again. . . . Basil Blackett is coming to tea, but he doesn't talk economics. He makes me tell him about Abelard instead.

Work and parties are inextricably mixed in Helen's letters, perhaps because she had no time to enter into the lives of people with little or no literary interests or tastes, though she did not entirely despise publicity values. To her

the W. B. Yeats' party was good but rather a strain, for he was full of a new Indian saint whose autobiography is to be published this week as he is now in London. Though we all listened dutifully, I'm afraid Yogi leaves me cold. However, W.B. was extremely kind to me, and saw me home and was frightfully interested in *Abelard*. I wanted him to make Robin Flower a member of the Academy, but he said he was too much the scholar, and not creative.

Last night at the Blacketts I didn't expect to enjoy it at all, but loved it. I was talking for a good while to Sir John Chancellor, who was Governor of Southern Rhodesia and then of Palestine in the recent troubles. I told him all about Jack, and he said he really began forestry in Rhodesia. . . . I always like mentioning Jack to the great ones, for the greater they are they never forget a name. (Basil says Chancellor is really a first class administrator.)

Much the same comment was applied to Sir Ronald Storrs, with whom Helen lunched, only he left her with Jack's name and address in his notebook, and a postscript adds that: 'Basil is to be in Livingstone in about six weeks time, and says if Jack could manage to be there he'd love to see him.'

After a bout of fatigue, aggravated by Professor Gregory Smith's death, Helen tells Meg:

Then Gregory died – they rang up to tell me. You know how one grieves for the dead who were thwarted in their lives, and I was haunted too by the pitiful patience of his eyes. Mercifully,

I had gone very steadily to see him of late. Saintsbury, bless him, was furious about the poor notice in *The Times* and is writing one himself.

Saturday was a dreadful day – a lecture on Alcuin, at Maidstone to the Classical Association, back about 6 o'clock. Changed in a bathroom at Victoria Station, and took taxi to Press Club, somewhere off Fleet Street. But it was one of the nights of my life. Charming chairman of Club, Colin Brooks, who did one of the best reviews of *The Wandering Scholars*: also my fellow guest, Sir Josiah Stamp, who is stout and twinkling, was excessively gallant in his speech, and told them about Baldwin at Queen's (he was there): 'If you had heard, as I did, the roars of applause that greeted her name, it would have left you in no doubt that she was Ulster's darling. Now that I have seen her I am not surprised.'

But by the time I got home you could have lifted me on a shovel. Stamp told me he thought Baldwin's speech was on the wireless in Belfast, but I don't suppose you heard it? I now have cold feet at the thought of it and wish I had refused. I think every college and university in England must now have asked me to read them a paper. The last was St. Andrew's, but I couldn't face it this year.

I am really looking forward to the long winter for work. I must lecture in Birmingham on translation, for the Classical Association and before that in Liverpool.

When winter came Helen's creative spirit rose again. She hopes for a visit from Meg, begs her to come over, saying:

I've just been trampling through the work, cutting like a sewing-machine, and the almost Trappist silence of it is like cool water on my head. . . . And all day yesterday I sat in this queer, lighted room, and saw a light moving outside, till at last in the evening I trekked across Primrose Hill to St. Mark's. They had candles and incense and a procession, and it was all 1000 years old, down to the sanctified stupidity on the priest's face. I'll never be a Catholic, but I'd never get my work done if I didn't now and then dive into that strange divine sea. This time I came up with a translation of Abelard.

> How mighty are the sabbaths,
> How mighty and how deep,
> That the high courts of heaven
> To everlasting keep.
>
> What peace unto the weary,
> What pride unto the strong,
> When God in whom is all things,
> Shall be all things to men.
>
> Jerusalem is that city
> Whereof the gate is peace,
> A peace that is surpassing
> And utter blessedness.
> There finds the dreamer waking
> Truth beyond dreaming far.
> Nor is the heart's possession
> Less than the heart's desire.

Some weeks later, after several meetings with Gustav Holst, she says:

> I haven't written any more of *Abelard*, busy with other jobs, like trying to alter the words of 'How mighty are the Sabbaths' to fit Gustav Holst's tune. He wants it for regular congregational singing, and some of the later lines are accented differently from the line in the first verse for which his tune was written. It's very difficult. For instance, 'There finds the dreamer waking Truth beyond dreaming far' has a lovely full note on the '*be*(yond)' which sounds ridiculous. But it took me about a week to write that verse at all, so it isn't hopeful.

Helen also corresponded with Dr Dwelly, the first Dean of Liverpool Cathedral, who wanted her hymn to be sung to the tune of 'All glory, laud and honour', with a two-line refrain after each verse. She felt any chorus effect was out of place and would not consider the idea.

The Irishman, George William Russell, poet, painter, economist and journalist, always known as 'AE', wrote stimulating letters to Helen before and after each of her books. As early as 1930 he is urging her to go ahead with the story of Héloise and Abelard:

> I read long ago the marvellous letters of Héloise, and I could not bear George Moore's tampering with the tale. He was not equal to imagining so much beauty and passion. The truth is that George Moore had really no passion in his writing. It all seems put on from the outside. Abelard gives opportunity for a great study in psychology.

The progress of Helen's novel was slow and fitful. References in letters to Meg are brief until in the autumn of 1932 she writes:

> I'm at the heresy hunt chapter now, and enjoying its malice – a great relief from the wild tragedy of the others. But I've had to read a lot of Abelard's theology to get into the heresy business – a difficult one technically. I wish I could read you what I've written, for it has knocked everything else from my head. . . . Darling, all this seems so remote from Killy and makes me homesick even for the smell of the hen-houses and the morass outside. It's so much more real life, but thank God, I have it and you always in the background.

Then a little later:

> I'm sitting by the fire for an hour or so, and then going out to dinner with Gustav Holst, a little slack but happy, for I finished a chapter yesterday – the dreadful one of Abelard's betrayal. And I actually did another this morning between breakfast and three o'clock – his determination to go into the

cloister and send Héloise too. That finishes Book II of the novel. There will be only three chapters in Book III, the great heresy hunt, Abelard's reconciliation down in the woods at Nogent, where you and I went, and one last chapter between old Gilles de Vannes and Héloise. . . . I almost begin to hope that it may be done by Christmas. It's marvellous having practically nothing to do but this one thing, except a little reading for Constable – none of the awful writing up books for jackets and such.

No news, darling. Basil* has gone, with a final box of lovely chrysanthemums before he sailed. I shall miss him badly, that massive kindness and goodness and above all his everlasting interest in Abelard.

By dint of refusing to review, and curtailing evening gaieties, Helen was able to let herself go and to dive into the depths of her perceptive involvement with Abelard, rising gasping to the surface to report each advance to Meg (her first major step was delayed it seems):

I have been very stupid for a day or two, and though I got exactly what I wanted to say in the chapter on Sunday, going down to Savernake in the train, I couldn't get it down until today. Now it is coming beautifully, but, alas, old Mayne turned up at 12, and bang went everything. However, now it has begun, I'm not afraid.

Next:

I don't think I got out of my chair unless to put coal on the fire, looked up at half past one and thought 'Better eat something', but relapsed again, and next time I looked the chapter was finished, and it was ten past four. I think myself it is the best thing I have ever done, but I'm still shaking with it. Honestly, Peg, it leaves you as if you'd had flu. But it is one of the high

* Sir Basil Blackett met Jack in Livingstone, Northern Rhodesia, and gave him an introduction to Government House which delighted Helen.

jumps safely over – there will be easier going now till the night of his mutilation. After which I expect to be wheeled about in a go-cart. I wish I could read it to you. I have seen how the new chapter is to go, but I shan't tackle it for a day or two – till my head rights itself.

And the next step is:

The chapter in the woods is all but finished. Only one chapter left to do. It almost makes me solemn: only I am convinced that I'll go on to do the letters and documents and pieces of his best prose, with a long introduction, so that I shan't be lonesome.

Then:

Darling, that chapter is written, and I think I'll put off beginning the last one till Monday. Queer, but I feel as if the best thing I've ever written, or ever will write, is now over. I've always known that that chapter of the discovery of God would be the hardest to do, and that if I made it insincere or sentimental it would be worse than useless. Now it's done, and I can't ever write anything like it again, because it seems to have used up all the knowledge I have. And I felt for so long that once *Abelard* was written the thing for which I was born would be done. Not that I'm in any mood to say the *Nunc Dimittis*. But just it's queer.

Paul Henry is taking me out to dinner tonight. I went to his private view and there were a lot of people there and I was made a great fuss of by everybody, which pleased me well.

And finally:

I don't know what I would do without your letters. I've written something about Héloise coming into the room to see old Gilles de Vannes in the last chapter, older, sadder, but with 'eyes that seemed to open the gates of mercy for mankind'. Yours are rather like that.

Och darling, it's finished! I finished it last night. Only in the rough of course, so that that shadow will still go with us for a long time yet. I felt more than ever writing the last page that this is not the end, but the end of one stage of the journey.

And then, as luck would have it, I crept downstairs at eleven, after writing that last page to look for letters, and found one from Maude telling me that Enid Starkie was knocked down by a bus in Oxford and is in the Acland Nursing Home with concussion, and worrying frightfully about her *Baudelaire* which Constable refused, and would I please send the MS on at once. And I had sent it registered a week ago. Luckily I have the registration receipt, though I have a sinful trick of throwing them away.

CHAPTER XI

Peter Abelard

To a supreme degree Helen possessed the art of opening the heart: into each of her characters she wrote herself, predominantly through Abelard, Then Héloise through Abelard's eyes, then Gilles de Vannes – the only person created out of her own imagination to be a link throughout the book. Her version is not fiction: every character (except Gilles), and every incident come from Latin sources which she translated or adapted, down to Thomas, Thibault's lame duck.

Her letters reveal how her mind worked; how when she saw similar characteristics in her friends and acquaintances she impulsively flattered them by endowing them with the names of characters from her novel. (She admits herself that Basil Blackett was the only one she called 'Abelard'.)

Some handwritten sheets of her original drafts have an interest all their own. Her immense carefulness over every sentence, every word she wrote, is shown in the innumerable corrections, erasures and alterations, all of them tending to brevity and refinement. Pre-eminently she desired to give the whole of herself; all her basic emotional intuitions, all her sublimations and all her acquired knowledge. Then, at a more practical level, she regarded the book as a tribute to two men – Professor Saintsbury and Professor Gregory Smith, whose influence and friendship had guided her through her prolonged formative years. The former especially had given her his eyes and his ears to appreciate to the full, first in Latin and then in French, the supreme virtue of controlled simplicity to produce effective meaning and enduring beauty. The poet in her had responded; her scholarship and her perceptive, penetrative compassion functioned together to produce a novel of classic quality. That Saintsbury died in 1933, just a few weeks before *Peter Abelard* was published, remained an abiding grief to her.

The fate of her proposed translation of Abelard's letters is not known. There are references to her working on them, and to her intention to conclude the tragedy of his and Héloise's lives in a second volume. Certainly she often talked about their final years. Gilles de Vannes was to be alive at the beginning – 'which would make the book a much happier one'. And Héloise's last words on her deathbed were to be, 'Christ have mercy on all young lovers.'

So *Peter Abelard* was written and the manuscript safely delivered to Constable's, and Helen, who was her own severest critic, sat back waiting with anxious impatience for the reactions of those she respected most, and then with lesser impatience for the verdict of professional reviewers.

She was, of course, sure of Meg's approval, and her reply was simply: 'If it weren't for you, I think three-quarters of the sweetness would go out of success. You are my acid test.'

Then she copied a letter from Michael Sadleir and enclosed it:

> You know he had seen nothing of it, and only got a copy of the typescript from me on Saturday to take home with him. . . . I think you'll take back any misgiving you've ever had about old Michael. And he wrote to O.K.: 'I have just written to Helen, I hardly know what I said. The thing is a miracle. It is the kind of book that only happens once in a generation.' Darling, calm yourself, and don't take it all too seriously, for it will likely get lots of crabbing. But some people love it, just as you and I do. . . . And yet already I am beginning to see tremendous things in a possible sequel. You know what we saw on the steps of the château at the Paraclete – the winding road and Abelard, coming back to her in that slow black procession, dead.
>
> Before I do the next novel you and I will have to travel down to Cluny, where Abelard took refuge, where there is a tremendous abbey; and to Sens where he was condemned as a heretic, where there is a marvellous cathedral. And this time we'll go to Père Lachaise in Paris, because it seems they have kept the actual tomb in which his body was first laid, down at

Châlons: and the effigy on it is believed to be Abelard. A face keen, thin, very like Dante's. And maybe we'll do the pilgrimage up through France from Cluny, as Peter the Venerable did it, to bring his body home.

Michael Sadleir's letter follows dated 10th February, 1933.

My dear Helen,

It is almost impossible to write to you about *Peter Abelard* without the sort of hyperbole which we are not nowadays permitted. Of course I expected great things, but *nothing* – nothing approaching what I found. The experience of reading it has been so terrific that I still feel all exalted and shaken, and will only say that you have written – I think – the most beautiful story I ever read.

Queer that one can go through life, tasting it, chewing the sweet and spitting out the bitter, living with one's stomach and one's brain: and when one might reasonably think all heat of the blood and folly of impulse were past (at any rate from history) – to have the heart torn out of your breast for two creatures a thousand years away.

Forgive the paraphrase, but that is how it is.

MICHAEL

A letter from another partner and the general effect at Constable's are reported to Meg:

They are awfully excited about the novel at the office. Sardonic Martha Smith read it and wept, and finally said: 'that if *that* wasn't a success, Constable's had better quit publishing and open a butcher's shop.'

The excitement mounts. Jacket to be designed by the man who did the marvellous woodcuts for Shaw's *Black Girl*. I saw him yesterday: and he told me he would like best to illustrate the novel right through, and that he couldn't put it down. But he's going to do Abelard leaning against the window with the moonlight outside and his arms stretched along the crossbars of

> the window. Do you remember the chapter he is in a devil's mood, and Gilles watching him thinks: 'God have mercy, it's a crucified Apollyon'? Now they are choosing type and so on. Then it will go to press and the proofs will be sent to the Book Society. I don't think for one moment they will choose it, but O.K. says grimly he'll give them a chance. Viner, our London traveller, is nearly off his head.

In the same letter Helen refers to her brother-in-law's disapproval. She is not upset or angry: her comment is simply: 'I told Ellis what *you* said – "with passion and amazement, borne on a tide that was beyond bar or delay". Strange about Daddy. But he is, after all, a generation further back than we are, and they used to think *Jane Eyre* immoral, and, I suppose *Antony and Cleopatra* too.'

And a fortnight later:

> The Times Book Club's *first* order is for 300 copies, not a bad start. And the reviews this weekend are just marvellous, and O.K. rang up almost trembling with excitement. He says *The Times* is their barometer and has ordered another 250 today. This means it's well away. Everybody is prancing, and I am so happy you are going to be here just for the beginning.

'AE' wrote sheets to Helen about her book, but he says himself that he is rambling egotistically, so it becomes a question of 'all or nothing' and two short paragraphs must suffice:

> It was most kind of you to send me your beautiful story. I can see how you have lived into it as if you were a contemporary, as indeed you may have been in some deep of your being. There is an Everliving in which past, present and future are one, and when we brood on the past it may be our own intensity brings us to live in that we brooded upon. It's not only in vision we revisit the past; our hearts may sink into it and know what others have known. This is a kind of faith with me.

> I have not written as I should about your book, but have let my thought run away about it. But you will forgive me.

However he also says in another letter:

> I am very glad you thought the review of your book interesting. I looked about to find the most competent reviewer I could, and chose Gerard Murphy who had, I found, made some study of his own of the literature you deal with. I thought of reviewing it myself simply as poetry, but felt that such a review would be unjust, when in addition to lovely verse, there was the aspect of scholarship to be taken into account, and I am no scholar in anything. I thought it a beautiful book and tried to do the best for it.

The success of *Peter Abelard* continued to be phenomenal. Constable brought out three editions in the first six months: American publishers came over to see it and secure contracts: it appeared as far away as New Zealand, as near as France.* Helen tells Meg:

> *Peter Abelard* is getting marvellous reviews in Germany. O.K. says the best literary journal there calls it 'The greatest novel of the Middle Ages ever written'. And as you can't say its doctrines are peculiarly Nazi, there must be some of the old romantic fire still. O.K. was almost purple with pleasure reading the huge advertisement page that my publisher sent me, for paper after paper went off the deep end, and I think he felt that the spirit in what is after all his father's fatherland is living yet.

Helen gave a small dinner-party in a restaurant, inviting such friends as Ellis and Harriet Roberts, Charles and Hilda Morgan, Stephen Gwynn, Mrs E. V. Lucas, Arthur Quiller-Couch and

*Translated and published in Denmark, 1934; in Germany, 1935; Czechoslovakia, 1937; Norway, Sweden, Finland, Spain and Portugal after the war; finally in Poland in 1953.

Storm Jameson. And she herself attended every type of social function, mostly luncheons, dinners, and receptions. And reviews became more and more laudatory. It was not very long before she admits:

> I'm almost distracted with pleasant things – lunch tomorrow with Walter de la Mare and Charles Morgan to meet G. K. Chesterton and I refused to dine tonight to meet Anthony Asquith again, for I am so tired. Dining at the Blackett's next week. Basil here yesterday, and clean off the deep end about *Abelard*.
>
> I love you and I *ache* for Killy. I don't know what it is about that house, but I'd be grateful now even for a little breath from the silo. Must stop, I'm to lecture – Alcuin again, and to the Irish Literary Society on Saturday.

A few days later she and O.K. dined at the Ivy with her American publisher and then went on together to a reception at Londonderry House.

> Lady Londonderry had said a 'small party', and so it was in numbers, but it seemed entirely composed of members of the Cabinet. The first person I saw on the stairs was Neville Chamberlain; and once inside O.K. said: 'There's Baldwin', and I said: 'There's Ramsay', and I introduced him to Baldwin, and he introduced me to Ramsay Macdonald, who looked exhausted and sad but extraordinarily distinguished. He told me he had given away three copies of the *Medieval Latin Lyrics*, and I promised him the *Scholars*. And Baldwin came over and said: 'When am I ever going to see you?' And finally: 'Will you come and have breakfast with me some morning? It's the only time I have to myself. . . .' And he came back before I left and said he would write and fix it up.

One more extract about festivities:

> I went to the Londonderrys with Sir William Rothenstein and

> enjoyed it enormously, just as a kind of Lord Mayor's show – the men in court dress, and the women superb. And Londonderry himself pursued me to tell me he had done a dreadful thing. He had cut three pages out of the book (*Peter Abelard*), so that he could carry them about. And was proceeding to further speech, when Palmstierna, the Swedish ambassador, literally grabbed him from me with: 'That's enough, Londonderry, I also love her!' So, my dear, a *very* agreeable evening. And I had been dreading it.
>
> I'm going to the Ellis Roberts for the weekend, dining with the Hudsons on Tuesday, and with Frances Blackett to meet Elizabeth Haldane (who wrote the '*Mrs. Gaskell*' that you read) on Wednesday. I seem to spend most of the morning saying: 'I'm so sorry I can't come'. But it is all rather fun, and that tonic is excellent.

From a practical and financial angle too the tonic was far beyond Helen's expectations, and she reported in another letter:

> The first edition is up in price already. Enid Starkie couldn't get one in Oxford, so I went to Ward's in Baker Street. They had one copy of the first that they took out of a drawer – 'But the price is up already, you know. It's impossible to get.' And Bumpus is begging for them from Constable's and can't get them.

So the year A.D. 1933 passed out for Helen in the rosy light of a *succès fou* for her novel.

CHAPTER XII

The Fateful Mistake

The first half of 1934 gives a picture of Helen's success very similar to 1933, full of pleasing invitations all socially and academically gratifying:

Almost demented, but awfully cheerful and not tired. . . . English Association dinner great fun – made really beautiful speech, I think, and lapped up vast lots of cream from other speakers. . . . Invited by the Londonderrys to *the* party of the season on Tuesday – the great party for the Conference, to meet the Prince of Wales and the Duke and Duchess of York. Nice of them and I've accepted, but I don't believe I'll ever have the courage to go, and in the crush won't even be noticed.

Was at Rothenstein's party at the Tate Gallery. Baldwin opened the Burne Jones private view, and he was a dear to me, and we are to meet when the Conference is over. Rothenstein is just dizzy about *Abelard*. But then he says it is like a new way of living. Darling, it's a crazy life!

Canterbury was really a treat when I got there, but I was never so dizzy with a lecture in all my life. It went off awfully well, and the man I was scared of, Dr. Jenkins, who was chairman and a great medievalist, said he hoped I'd publish it. . . . That night was just straight out of *Barchester Towers*: I was staying with the Gardiners, Precincts 14 – just under the shadow of the Cathedral, and only for Canon Gardiner who is 73 and quite round and says with a deep chuckle now and then, 'quite a Precinct remark', I might have squealed. His friends say that

that is why he is not a bishop: the twinkle is too unruly. He is the kind of person at whose feet you and I roll at sight. . . . A faultless house, 17–18th century, Chippendale, lots of silver boxes about, all very bright, a maid who unpacks one's meagre belongings and houses them in a bow-fronted chest of drawers (very inconvenient in a hurry), fire in one's room, claret and port, the incredibly sweet chime of the Cathedral bell. And the Cathedral itself next morning . . . the only English Cathedral I know that makes me think of Chartres.

Then a week or two later:

Just back from breakfast with Baldwin. A lovely quiet room, and a little round table just for myself, himself and the man who is secretary of the Pilgrim Trust (Tom Jones) and runs a very luxurious private press,* for which he wants me to do a translation. And I told S.B. the story about Jack and the catalpa tree. It moved him, really moved him, and he just sat silent with that dear 'learned Pig' face of his all softened. I told it to Basil Blackett at tea yesterday, and he is going to use it in a speech. Darling, could you find him the exact letter; I know Jack's words will be better than anybody's. He has a kind of magic simplicity.

And when I came away, Baldwin got me into my coat and said: 'You'll come and do this often? It's done me a world of good.' He said it twice.

In the meantime Helen was also lecturing extensively and doing work for Constable's, but in such spare moments as were left, she could retreat into her own small flat and collect delightful tales of the mutual charities between saints and beasts from the fourth to the twelfth centuries. They are translated without sophistication from the original Latin.

Robert Gittings adorned the book with attractive woodcuts, and Constable & Co. published it in 1934 under the title *Beasts and Saints*.

*Greg-y-Nog, Merioneth, Wales.

Here is one more typical letter written while Helen was on the crest of the wave of success:

> . . . I was away for the weekend at the Greg-y-nog Press, to read poetry at the Memorial Festival for Elgar and Holst. The Press is partly run by Tom Jones, ex-Cabinet secretary, the dear little man I met at breakfast with Baldwin. It's a most lovely house in Wales, lapped in luxury, and exactly like something in *The Pilgrim's Progress*, including the two Davies sisters who own it, and who might be Mercy and Discretion. They are so good and so gentle, God bless them. They would like to work out some scheme that would endow me to do no more hack work at all. Meantime I have promised to translate the *Letters of Héloise and Abelard* for a superb Limited Edition – Japanese vellum and so on. . . . And *Abelard* goes on selling, and has begun in New Zealand.
>
> Went to a really delightful dinner, when the Rothensteins took me to the old Ranee of Sarawak (I suppose the only province where the Rajah is an Englishman). She is a magnificent old pillar of 82, like Trilby grown old, and devilishly witty; bolt upright in a high chair, no cushions, and an old butler calling her 'Your Highness'. She was just foolish about *Abelard*, and also very flattering about my personal appearance; an irresistible combination. . . . Then next day came a lunch, a large party at the Blacketts; and then tea at Lady Ottoline Morrell's, who has a kind of salon. She is full of teeth, dark, huge eyes, and thin but somehow lovable. 'AE' was there, and we almost huddled together. And through all this I was struggling to write a review of Michael Sadleir's *Blessington-d'Orsay*. It got finished at two in the morning on Friday. I crawled to bed, then got up, revised it and dashed down to *The Observer* in a taxi. . . . My depression was increased by feeling that it was a rather heavy review and poor Michael would be bitterly disappointed. Instead of which he met me yesterday clean off his head with pleasure and excitement.

Then in the summer of 1934 came a bolt from the blue. The

landlord of Helen's flat gave his tenants notice to quit, because all the houses in Ormonde Terrace came into a scheme for demolition, or conversion into a block of modern flats.

Helen's reaction – partly from having money to spare for the first time in her life – was totally unrealistic. Impulsively, with little or no forethought, she plunged into the purchase of an end-lease of thirty years' duration for a large and unwieldy house in Primrose Hill Road. She was mesmerised by its shabby walled-in garden, and its outlook on tall trees and glimpses beyond of green grass rising to the hill above. She insisted that they reminded her of Kilmacrew, and the idea of owning a house that would accommodate in London all her beloved family and still have bedrooms to spare, blinded her even to consideration of the amount of domestic staff necessary for the upkeep and running of a three-storeyed house with an outsize basement. All her efforts later to conquer the damp cold of the interior were sadly deficient, and permission to install overall central heating was refused (presumably because of dissatisfaction with the fabric or the shortness of the remaining lease).

Maude Clark, Helen's Somerville friend and fellow-countrywoman from Belfast, warned her openly and unequivocally of the mistake she was making; most forcibly from the point of view of the effect on her work. She would be distracted by domesticity, too absorbed in the care of tenants if she let off rooms, and of relations and friends who would take advantage of her hospitality. In fact, she would never write anything 'truly great' again. Helen was frightened, but unconvinced: it was enough for her that 'No. 32' reminded her of Kilmacrew.

Helen's niece, Mollie Martin, came over from Ireland to help in starting up the new home. She recollects that:

> AE was one of Helen's first guests at No. 32 Primrose Hill Road, and I remember so vividly AE, Helen, OK and I having coffee in that queer shabby garden. And Helen saying to AE wasn't it a nice house and didn't he like it? And AE scolding her for having bought it. 'You'll never be able to work again. The roof will leak, the bath taps will drip etc. Nobody who

works with their head should ever acquire property or possessions, they should live out of a suitcase.' Then he went on to lecture her about being a social success, and said that every dinner-party he was invited to, the bait to lure him was that Helen Waddell would be there. He wagged an admonitory finger at her and added: 'You watch or you will become nothing but a handshake and a brilliant talker, like James Stephens – that was what ruined him.' Even then I felt how right he was about the house.

But Helen tells Meg:

I have been so rushed and let the days go by. The house is a dear, a little like Killy in its ring of giant trees, and, I am afraid the same queer power of absorbing. . . . Mollie is an absolute darling. Don't know what I should have done without her. I am just dying for you to see it all. Builders and painters due for about another month. I am taking darling garden room after all with bathroom next door in basement. I couldn't sleep in the large dining-room on street for anything. It was like the Euston Hotel somehow, not too noisy but very public so I gave it to the Beneys* . . .

O.K. came for one night to sleep in a bare room on a makeshift bed, just Sunday night on his way back from Savernake. He adored it so he asked to stay on, never slept so well for years. Now he encamps upstairs with crumbs of furniture stolen from Rosamond and me and is as gay as can be. Maude's brother has been here, full of advice about the garden. Altogether we are having the time of our lives – only I have been trying to do the Introduction to the *Beasts* in odd hours, and I got a head like a hot oven and have finally given up until next week.

Helen describes the house in detail in several letters but

*The Beneys, husband and wife who were in Ormonde Terrace and who agreed to run Helen's house when she moved.

apparently never realised how she was complicating her own life by letting O.K. live there too.

To Meg a week later:

> You have been dreadfully neglected, but I've been barely human, and only got the *Beasts* to press yesterday. I wrote and scrapped and re-wrote, and though the house is the dearest and best-natured in the world, the muddles of painters and plumbers and electricians all doing the opposite of what they were told, and always putting the wrong things in the wrong place, were endless till you never knew what they'd do next. And no Mrs. Beney yet. . . . I got hopeless about the *Beasts* in the end, but I think it's good now.

From the moment Mrs Beney arrived she complained the work was too much for her, and by September she and her husband had left.

Helen's courageous spirit and her urge to write at any cost met hurdles time after time. The world was at her feet, *asking* to give her publicity, honours, adulation, all its most sought-after gifts, but it could not give her peace of mind or the quiet of a heart that accepts. She tore herself to pieces for tranquility to write in an understaffed, awkward household. She was hospitable to a fault and filled whatever rooms she happened to have vacant not only with the family from Kilmacrew, but with almost anyone who appealed to her. Finally she added to her labours by deciding that eggs were a necessity for O.K., and had hen-houses erected, and spent hours herself fixing wire-netting round suitable patches for runs, or as defence against errant hens who wanted to explore her few pathetic flowerbeds, or cluck their way up the iron stairs to an open French window and lay their eggs on her drawing-room chairs.

Letters began to arrive in praise of *Beasts and Saints*. One of the first came from Rose Macaulay. She and Helen had become great friends and had discussions together after publication about each of their books. Rose Macaulay was fascinated by the *Beasts*, and by way of reply sent Helen a copy of her own *Minor Pleasures of Life*.

AE sent Helen a Christmas card he had drawn for her, and wrote on it: 'A Lion meditating in the desert after partaking of a saint. Notice God-given halo.' A note written on the back of the card reads: 'Forgive me for petulance about the Saints. They are too much with us in Ireland, and I forget that elsewhere some might deserve the name.'

And Walter de la Mare ends his letter of praise for the book: 'If only some of your Saints would come back and take the place of some of our Sages! Aren't you wearied to death of quick wits, slick thinking and acid tongues?'

Finally Stanley Baldwin's letter:

> What a lovely present! You do indeed make and cause to be made such delightful things. 'When I consider how my life is spent' etc., grinding out platitudes for deaf ears, I envy you. I have already plunged into your tales and I am entranced by the very first one. I shall work on to the Lion in time, though I looked up your reference.
>
> It is curious, but I have always lived with St. Jerome, that delicious picture of him reading with a large pair of bedroom slippers neatly placed by his side.
>
> It would be such a pleasure to see you again and to learn through what jolly seas you are voyaging at present.

A further revelation of Helen's scholarly mind is in a Christmas letter to Basil Blackett:

> I suddenly began translating the Latin thing Milton wrote '*In Adventum Veris*' when he was twenty, all for the sake of one line ending . . . '*sera crepuscula surgunt*.' 'So through the meadows, when the late twilight riseth.' *Surgunt* for twilight is wonderful. But one piece went into lyric, and you shall have it. It is Earth pleading with her lover, the sun, not to spend his night with the Sea. (I always thought Milton had a fine sensual imagination, and the Latin poem proves it.)

Wearied with climbing the high cliffs of heaven,
Love, wouldst thou rest?
Still must thou plunge in the dark sea at evening?
Close thine eyes on my breast.

Must thou go down to the sea in the twilight?
Cool are the trees,
Fresh is the grass, and over wet roses
Light whispers the breeze.

Salt on thy lips the Iberian waters,
Seas of the west.
Softer thy sleep on the cold dewy grasses.
Close thy eyes on my breast.

H.W.

Probably the influence of Saintsbury's recent death had taken Helen back to Milton. It was he who had judged her thesis for the D.Litt. degree that Belfast had given her, when her theme had been 'An Aspect of the poet Milton'.

The festivities that preceded her Christmas visit to Kilmacrew were obviously appreciated:

. . . I have had a marvellous week though – AE on Saturday, lunch and again dinner, and yesterday lunch with Bernard Shaw: and I feel rather as if I now know the two greatest men there are. AE has grown into a saint, with a head like an old Zeus – curly Greek philosopher's head, old and wise and so gentle. And the stories he told, comic and ironic, and every now and then a flash of poetry, his own or remembered. I looked up his book after he had gone away, the bit where he says that one must not fight with violence, even for truth. 'I learned that if we are gentle enough, God will give us a star to lead us.' He is like that.

You know I always looked askance at G.B.S. There was no real surrender in me to him, except at *St. Joan*. But the old man himself has just bowled me over. As thin as a fishing rod, and as sardonic as a knife; but at the back of him such vast ironic kindness, and a kind of mental integrity and simplicity. His wife is cracked about *Abelard*, and G.B.S. has now begun it, dragooned into doing it, he grumbled to me, because everybody yelled at him to read it.

'That's a lie,' said I, 'you wanted to read it.' He scowled at me. 'How do you know?' 'Because otherwise you'll have to admit you were bullied into doing *anything* against your will.' He was enchanted. The only way to get on with him is to tell him the absolute truth, as recklessly as possible. Then you see him kindle.

CHAPTER XIII

The Shadowed Year

The next year, 1935, was a chequered one for Helen. Her play, *The Abbé Prévost*, flared in her mind again. O.K. published a small but beautiful limited edition of it, and the chance to get it produced occurred. Helen writes to Meg: 'Shaw told O.K. that he couldn't be sure the play would really "get across", that he couldn't judge how far his own liking for Prévost and knowledge of *Manon* tricked him, but that he was the "hardened professional" and that his wife was terribly moved by it.'

Meg was staying at Primrose Hill when *The Abbé Prévost* was first staged by the Croydon Repertory Company in May 1935, and on the following Sunday it was produced in London by Michael MacOwan at the Arts Theatre Club in Great Newport Street.

The production was not an unequivocal success. It is very hard to apportion the blame fairly. Better actors might have brought life into their parts, particularly that of the hero, the Abbé himself, and Lenki the heroine, both of whom were unconvincing. But as the dialogue – lovely prose as it was – never inspired a single moment of irresistible emotion, one is bound to conclude that the author failed too.

Basil Blackett and his sister were dumbly depressed for Helen's sake, but fortunately others were less disappointed, or were better able to enthuse out of politeness. After much clapping and calls for the author, all were laughing, and could thoroughly enjoy Helen squeezing herself along the front rows kissing each person in turn, stopping for breath and gasping: 'Now who haven't I kissed?' and being answered by cries of 'Me!' and 'Me!' and 'Me!' The evening ended with a happy party at Helen's house, sitting on the floor, feeding on sausages and beer. All were gay and lighthearted, all were friends and worshippers.

Helen never attempted another play, but for years she entertained the idea of adapting *Peter Abelard* for the stage: indeed she must have done some work on it as she promised the name part to a friend, Robert Donat.

Very shortly after the production of *The Abbé Prévost* Helen was on her way to New York where Columbia University was to confer on her an honorary D.Litt. degree.

On board the S.S. *Berengaria* she sends Meg a note: 'I feel if you had been here it would have done you all the good in the world. . . . I am leaving all woes behind. And greatly cheered this morning by Lenki's gay small face . . . last news about play is that two theatre managers and two film companies are demanding scripts of it. I got that just as I was going on board.'

By the time the ship docked at New York, Helen's resilient spirit had been entirely restored. As usual everyone felt her attraction, which she found 'vastly agreeable', and she adds: 'The Commodore urged me to come back with him today, and let the degree go, as did also the Chief Steward.'

The long letters from 'The Deanery, Barnard College, Broadway' describe her impressions of New York:

> It is really being very peaceful. The Dean* is a darling, huge dark eyes put in with a smutty finger, half French, and very entertaining. She is giving a dinner-party for me tonight, but left me in great peace yesterday, only for eager members of the staff who called. . . . It is the sultry airless damp heat that almost makes one's lungs labour in breathing. It fell on us coming up the river, a fog as well, so that New York rose like a Byzantine island (it's like Paris, the kernel of the whole city with the river meeting at the prow), and the incredible skyscrapers looked in the mist like campaniles. In fact, my first impression of New York was an island of ancient churches with high bell-towers: and the sun flecked through the mist, and you

*Miss Virginia Gildersleeve.

saw the green roofs gleam like the greenish bronze you see on Notre Dame.

My D.Litt. gown is exactly what they want. The whole ceremony takes place in the open air, on the steps outside their old library which was once King's College founded by George II. The procession comes out of the Library down a long flight of stone steps and out on to a terrace made wider by a wooden stage, and there the Senate and the graduates sit, with old Murray Butler* in front of a gold statue of Alma Mater. It is a far cry from Durham Cathedral, but it is terribly exciting.

There was, however, another aspect of Helen's visit:

If only I could have written to you every night, you'd have kept some part of me; but it's about time I left New York.

Tuesday was the conferring: Wednesday lunch with Holt directors (the publishers), and a cocktail party which is only a blur of faces and voices. Next day Professor Byrne in high exaltation from eleven to four, and a visit to the Rockefeller Institute for the Humanities; home for two short hours to be teased by the Dean who watched me with extreme delight. Murray Butler said in her hearing that it was almost unprecedented to combine such scholarship with such charm, which Virginia said was very hard on the other women of his university. Then Barry arrived, rather in the mood of the Barcarolle, to which we agreed to set Swinburne's verses instead –

'A little while a little love.
The hour still for thee and me,
Who have not drawn the veil to see
If yet the heavens are lit above.'

And we set off, still under the whimsical eyes of the Dean, and down through Central Park, in an amazing sunset, with all the western side of those terrible Babylonish buildings one

*Nicholas Murray Butler, President of Columbia University and of Barnard College. Nobel Prize winner in 1931.

glory. And then to the Plaza, where Barry had not been since the war, and there had cocktails, then down on to the Rainbow Roof in the Radio City building – 80 storeys up – and dined somewhere in the sky above New York, all mist and lights at our feet. It was the kind of place where you dance in between the soup and fish, if you wish. I was by way of thinking it was very much better not, but the music was too good, and the cabaret dancing in between too incendiary. So we dined and danced there till midnight. And then on to the Casino – the Folies Bergères straight from Paris (very wicked but extremely lovely in pieces) – and long intervals for dancing. And so miles back to the Deanery, and walk for a while under the moonlight there in the Dean's garden, and a farewell worthy of Verona. (So like me, as Barry said next day, to bring the Romeo and Juliet madness upon a respectable Dean of Engineering in the garden of the Dean of a Women's College). For of course we met again next day. I packed all the morning, lunched with Miss Ogden-Reid who is supposed to be about the last stronghold of the aristocratic tradition of New York (Whitelaw Reid's daughter-in-law). Then on to Finley, now editor of the *New York Times*, to thank him for a charming leader on me in that morning's paper. We talked about an hour on a book he is doing called *The Desire of the Mind*, and, to the profound astonishment and respect of Virginia, he came suddenly down to the *Aquitania* that evening to bring me a book and bid me goodbye. He is supposed to be the busiest man in New York. Then I met Barry for tea, and he came on with me to a cocktail party at the Van Dorens (literary editor of *The Tribune*). Then back to a solitary and affectionate dinner with Virginia, who drove me down to the boat, and we ran into a gallant but desperate Barry, who had dashed down before his own train left, to say one last goodbye. So we saw off Virginia together – a straight-faced but twinkling Dean! As I pointed out to him earlier, there is a kind of curious delight in the 'without tomorrow, without yesterday'.

Well, well, I do confess that the *Aquitania* seemed a little rural and domestic after all this. But the morning after I arrived, I was suddenly almost enveloped in a bear's hug by Sir Josiah Stamp. But, my dear, how queer and grim life is. Some hours later I was sitting in a chair and observed Josiah sitting alone, looking rather ill and sad. Then he got up and began tramping up and down. I glanced up and smiled, and he came over to me and crushed a cable into my hand: 'Father died last night. Delaying funeral till Saturday.' I couldn't say anything – I just held his hand a minute against my face and went away. But the sight of him sitting there, with his hand over his eyes, remembering, remembering. . . .

I'm finishing this in a rather stuffy writing-room, but I don't want to go back on deck. All the bubbles in the champagne suddenly gone . . . don't think I am the vainest peacock to write all this nonsense about Barry – but to tell you the truth, I think it gave us both a kind of release: one grows so old and good and wise and bored. It's just – you know my old theory of the people who belong to me, and are bound to fall a little in love – more or less. It was like that. You recognize each other, almost at once. And it does nobody any harm, though it is just as well that this had to stop when it did. I gave him *The Lyrics* as a goodbye present: and got a wireless from him yesterday. It was a line from the poem Fortunatus sent to his friend:

> 'You at God's altar stand, His minister,
> And Paris lies about you, and the Seine,
> About this Breton isle the ocean
> Deep water and one love between us twain.'

It was the last line – and it is the absolute curtain for the last act.

On the voyage back to England Helen wrote what she calls 'a long queer poem on New York'. It was published by the Greg-y-Nog Press with a wood-cut impression by Stefan Mrozewski in December 1935. Opinions varied: its appeal is, perhaps, limited to the man for whom it was written and fails to reach most other readers, but there is no evidence that Helen sent it to Barry.

In her first letter to Meg after her return home, she writes:

I've written about ninety letters and dispatched half a dozen MSS, and I am now on *The Desert Fathers.* Last night at the Blacketts was great fun. Sir Robert Horne, Chancellor of the Exchequer, had rung up from the House that he couldn't come. The message, as delivered by Basil in full drawing-room was 'Robert says he would go through heaven and hell to sit under H.W., but daren't face his constituency if he shirks the Scottish Housing debate'. But I had Austen Chamberlain and just fell for him, the gentlest, most unselfish creature, and very funny about his legs when they made him a Knight of the Garter. 'If I had known H.M. would ever dream of giving me that, I'd have done something to develop the calves of my legs in my youth.' He is absolutely unlike the monocle-orchid photographs.

Helen had begun to work on *The Desert Fathers* before she went to America, and Basil Blackett shared her interest, as did Charles Morgan.

On August 15th, Sir Basil was fatally injured in a motor accident in Germany; it was a blow that shocked Helen deeply. Her first letter was to his sister Monica:

Monica, my darling, – Basil, our dear Basil. Oh my dear, whatever has been, a prince has fallen, a kind of lost archangel. And now not lost any more. It is not for nothing that he is the only man who was ever able to translate St. Peter Damian's '*Paradise*' – 'He hath turned from all that changeth to the changeless source of all'.

Darling, this house is ready for you any time, any hour – and we'll do anything you want. O.K.'s love and mine, my dear heart. O Monica, there must be the world to come. I always felt it of Abelard, and of Lear: why discipline so cruelly, and then kill, just when one might have begun to live? Unless one is beginning to live, being through the life that now is.

O Monica, it is as if one side of one's house had fallen down.

HELEN

The next day she wrote to Meg:

I think you will be nearly as sad as I am about our old Basil. There's been a motor accident in Germany, and he is dead. He was driving to Heidelberg to give a lecture at the University. And at a level-crossing a train smashed into his car. He died of internal haemorrhage about three hours after. He was conscious only for a few moments and spoke a little, but it was too faint for anyone to hear.

I can't talk about it. It's as if a wall of this house had fallen. O.K. is stricken. He goes about saying: 'Basil, Basil.' I think you know that after O.K. I cared more for him than for any man. I was never for a moment in love with him; but somehow I think he was my very blood-brother in the sense of spirit and heart: and he was Abelard. I used to call him that, even at a dinner-party – by mistake – just association. But for himself I think the lost archangel has got home. . . . My dear, I think I'll grieve for him until I die. To know that I'll never read him pieces of the new *Abelard*. But I'll dedicate it to his memory.

After the funeral she wrote:

It's been a dreadful week, and I couldn't get time to write. Monica left on Monday, and when she could she dashed up here, just to keep sane. Basil's ashes only came yesterday – a day after the funeral was fixed, and everything went wrong, and once Monica got O.K. to telephone to Germany for them. Beatrice (Basil's wife), they have kept dazed with drugs.

But yesterday the Memorial Service at St. John's, Smith Square, and the funeral at Highgate Old Cemetery were in some strange way transfigured. I have never felt Basil so radiantly alive. The service itself was a marvellous bit of prose. (Read it – I stole a copy for you.) But Chopin's Dead March at the last is hard to bear, and do you know, it seemed all wrong for him. The funeral at Highgate was just the family.

Two more of Helen's best friends were to die before the year was over, both from cancer: Maude Clark and AE. The former resigned from her post at Somerville College at the end of the summer term. Her doctors had diagnosed inoperable cancer. Maude must have asked Helen to tell her father as she herself had told no one at Oxford. After his visit Helen writes: 'Daddy Clark came and I told him about Maude. He was awfully gentle and good. I had a long letter from him afterwards: "Even our Lord said 'My soul is exceeding sorrowful', and He will not take it amiss that I suffer." '

Helen visited Maude in her Belfast home more than once, and was at Kilmacrew when she died in November, so there are no descriptive letters to Meg.

Cancer killed 'AE' more quickly. He was in a nursing-home at Bournemouth when he wrote his last letter to Helen towards the end of August 1935.

Dear Helen,

Thanks for your letter. It is you who are impish. The doctors held their last consultation over me this morning and told me my trouble was not curable by either medical or surgical means but it might be palliated by an operation which would relieve me somewhat, which operation I believe I am to undergo shortly. They give me about a year. Don't think I feel despondent or melancholy. I have done my work and have had many good friends and no bad ones so far as I know, and I believe in the great spiritual verities and am not in the least unhappy nor would I wish my friends to be. At present I am very feeble but they tell me after the operation I shall feel easier.

My regards to Kyllmann.

Helen writes a sad letter to Meg:

AE is very ill, and it is incurable. I got a letter from him on Wednesday: they operated that day, and it is malignant. I went down to the nursing-home at Bournemouth yesterday with O.K. AE wasn't able to see O.K., and me only for about two minutes, but he had begged to see me and they let him. Very thin and waxen and strangely young. I think he is dying, and it would be so much better because it will be in a few months anyhow. The surgeon said that he told AE before he operated that it would be only temporary, anyhow, but better for him now. AE, he says, never moved a muscle, or flickered: he discussed the whole thing tranquilly as if it were the tilling of a field. 'It was like a spirit talking about a body that it had no concern with,' the surgeon said, and he was so shaken by the sheer saintliness in the man that he had to make some excuse and leave him, or he would have broken down.

... I told AE I would never be without him.

'Light in valley . . . the twilight air
That has made anchorites of kings.'

The operation was beyond AE's strength, for still in August Helen and O.K. 'dashed across to Dublin for AE's funeral – he was awfully glad he (O.K.) went for he was the only man from this side. We crossed back by the next boat. But everybody crashed for O.K. Dulanty gave us dinner at Euston. AE just slept away.'

Helen wrote an obituary on Maude Clark for *The Times* that was greatly appreciated by her family, and also an article-length tribute to AE for a magazine.

Her tribute to Basil Blackett came two years later, after she had selected the best of his poems (translations from Greek and Latin, published in a limited edition by his family). A personal paragraph on the man himself has some marvellous prose in it, of the same lofty quality and standard that appear in her introduction to *The Desert Fathers*, which was occupying her mind at the time.

> To these four poets came a man of a thousand contradictions – a thousand warring impulses, of towering ambition and complete self-abnegation, a humanist tempted by asceticism, a conservative rooted in the past, driven by an arduous furor to amend the bitter present, a statesman without office, a heretic in finance whose heresy is now orthodoxy, a ruthless logical scientific brain overshadowed by the cloud of unknowing, a sceptic apprehended by God.

After all this Helen was exhausted and Mollie came over from Kilmacrew and took her for a short holiday to Northumberland, to Warkworth and Lindisfarne.

CHAPTER XIV

The Desert Fathers

The Introduction to *The Desert Fathers* was hailed by many critics as superlative prose; and many reviewers, including Evelyn Underhill, received the whole book as a feat of incomparable literature. Genius is as delicate as it is rare. Helen herself was awed by the *Vitae Patrum* (revised 2nd edition, Plantin Press, Antwerp, 1628) which was the main source of her tales.

In her opinion: '*The Desert Fathers* are a thousand times finer than I'd ever dreamed. The great folio lies on the oak chest in front of the side window, and small winds blow over the old 17th century pages: and I sit on a little stool before it, with my writing-block on my knee, and the days go by in a dream.' (This was the scene in Grace Henry's portrait, which though too elusive for reproduction remains the best likeness of Helen.)

The visit of a Belfast friend and novelist was reported to Meg: 'George Buchanan was here and I read him some of the Introduction. He almost wept with excitement, and says it's the best thing I've ever written. I can't believe it, for it was like breaking up the concrete.'

Interruptions, social and domestic, occurred every day. The former were often appreciated, as when Lady Londonderry 'rang up to ask me to dinner; the Archbishop of Canterbury, and she hopes, Stanley Baldwin, so I shall wear the grey chiffon frock. And so it goes.'

But domestic troubles increased, partly due to O.K's need of more care. He must have reached his seventies, and his inability to do anything for himself grew with each year that passed. Helen always put him first and was always gentle and patient. Her defence against the confusion in her own house was to rent an artist's studio on the Regent's Canal, where she could write in peace. In December 1935 she wrote to Monica Blackett:

> But oh the relief of really getting something decent written. . . . I have been blind and deaf and choked with the sand of the desert, and none of its springs, till yesterday when I finished in a kind of blaze. It was a sudden translation from the end of the *Paradiso*, the tercet beginning: '*Un punto solo m'e maggio letargo*' – I'd written 'each moment has its eternal freight' and then I saw this:
>
> 'One point of time hath deeper burdened me
> Than all the centuries that have forgot
> How Argo's shadow startled first the sea.'

Then an important academic date cropped up: 'So excited – new degree – St. Andrew's this time, Doctor of Laws. (I suppose LL.D. but they said it in full). They said Senate and Committee unanimous. I'm frightfully pleased, because they really are a medieval university; they've been there since 1120.'

As usual Helen was received with honour and friendship and responded with her usual gratitude and grace in spite of physical fatigue.

On her return she finished reading the proofs of *The Desert Fathers*, and Constable's brought out the book in April 1936. Helen tells Meg: 'I've had amazing letters about *The Desert Fathers*. I think I never had such letters, and I'm sending you a batch of lovely reviews too. . . . Have to go to Marlborough this weekend with Beatrice Blackett. O.K. agrees we'll go every Sunday to the sea. The last one made us feel ten dogs.'

Stanley Baldwin writes from 10 Downing Street:

> I have often wondered how you were faring, and you may imagine with what pleasure I received your letter and the proof volume on the last day of the Easter recess. It is a lovely book and I would like to talk to you about it. And bless you for your sympathetic and understanding words. I don't say I should ever fly to the desert, but I am overdue for a spell there!

This is in some ways as terrible a world as that from which your Desert Fathers fled: but my peace is not there.

My love to you, and my high regard.

S.B.

And six months later a letter from Mr and Mrs Max Beerbohm from Rapallo in Italy:

Indeed I am glad and for once proud of my 'wisdom' of having left this lovely work for a peaceful, an uninterrupted time. I am not sure that it was not just as well that I had to stay in bed for two days, so that nothing could come between me and its great beauty.

The writing is like bathing in a good, strong upholding sea. One is upheld and strengthened by its strength, soothed by its lovely rhythms and cadences, and borne along singing oneself. This is attainment, perfect presentation without intervention.

Can't you ever find yourself at the railway station at Rapallo, or can't we find you there and bring you here to a room that looks on the sea and that you wouldn't, I think, dislike?

Our love
Affectionately
Florence.

P.S. To me you are like Tyndale,* with the bishops thrown in. You're technically matchless.

Max

A letter to Meg at this period reveals the deep spiritual springs of the scholar's mind that fed Helen's perceptiveness, her compassion and her pen:

I made O.K. go away to Savernake just to sleep and slump, and stayed here myself. (Rosamond is away today to Czechoslovakia.) The house is very quiet – and I am so home-

*William Tyndale, *d.* 1536, translator of the Bible.

sick for you. . . . Then, in the middle of indexing *Mr. Cole* I reflected how lucky beyond all women we are to be so fond of each other. Because if one loves, one really isn't lonely: it is the unloving heart that is always cold, and has no fire to warm itself at. 'Beloved, let us love one another, for love is of God: and he that loveth is born of God and knoweth God.' Don't tell me there are theological explanations of it – that the love must be 'in Christ'. He that loveth . . . knoweth God. Which means that it is when one's heart goes out to anything, it is, in that moment, close to God. And what if it were really true, that the power at the back of all this cruel universe were love as we know it. It's no wonder Dante said when he had that vision of 'love that moves the sun and the stars' that it was 'tanto ottraggio' a kind of outrage on his being. For to come within the least whisper of it is to leave one gasping.

It is good to be alone like this: to know that I shall be alone till tomorrow gives me a kind of key to peace. I begin to see what happened to Abelard, when he saw the Holy Ghost was love, and that the whole world lay in it, moved by it, the love of God the Father and God the Son.

One writes it, and it is trite – the familiar commonplace that we have heard from our cradles. But if ever one comes within its breath, it is so terrible that one almost looks about for familiar little shelters of noise and buses to shut out the stars.

'There shall no man see Me, and live.' And so the Son of Man comes eating and drinking, it being the only way in which human beings can endure to apprehend God. Reading this through, it seems trite and worn. It is no wonder the old Fathers could never get into words their times of vision. By the time it gets into the second volume of Abelard, it may have found some way of getting down on paper.

In December 1936, the reaction of Helen and O.K. to the abdication of Edward VIII manifests her emotional approach and O.K.'s sentimental one, both equally fundamental in the heredity of their nationalities – Irish and German. They were staying at

Kilmacrew when the news first broke, and both sent passionate telegrams on behalf of Edward to the Prime Minister.

After their return to London, Helen wrote to Meg:

> Always after I have left you I want to write to you every day: and then the tide of work rises and I disappear. But I must send this small note.
>
> O.K. very well and cheerful: he has written a marvellous letter to Stanley Baldwin which I'll try to get a copy of. I wrote to him myself today; a difficult letter to write: 'I began many letters to you, and could not go on, for there was so much bitterness in my heart. Never against you, but against mankind. Their cruelty, their fickleness, their smugness in the face of tragedy. Your final speech was like a mountain. But the days before it were poisoned to me by the slow distilled venom of the leaders in *The Times*. What blackness of heart was in Geoffrey Dawson, wounded vanity or secret spite, that made him pursue that haunted figure, that 'Love in desolation masked'? It was anguish to me to read them. But three people in that tragedy redeemed it: the lad that is gone, the brother who succeeded him with such heartbroken chivalry, and you that were a father to them both.'

Apart from the many social invitations Helen received, she was often asked to write or speak for fund-raising for charities. Usually she refused, but when Rosamond Tweedy, who was Secretary of the Over Thirty Association and had a flat in her house, repeatedly begged her to read poetry, she did agree. Meg immediately gets a letter:

> If you can possibly get away, there's one thing you must come over for. You remember the scheme that Jelly d'Aranyi and I were to give a kind of recital for Rosamond's poor Over Thirties? Nancy Astor was to house it, but is in mourning for her sister – and finally I pulled up my socks and asked Lady Londonderry. She rang me up next morning. 'But of course, Charles and I would do *anything* for you. What about May 3rd,

the night before our official Coronation Reception? The season opens with that – on May 4th – and you'll just catch them all the night before, when there's nothing to go to', – and Rosamond's gloss 'then the ones who *aren't* asked to the reception can pretend they were, because they've come to Londonderry House.' And Adila Fachiri is going to play with Jelly, and I'll read 'New York City' and one or two other things. And you *must* come with O.K. and Mollie and sit on a little gold chair, and see Londonderry House at its best.
P.S. Dinner at the Ivy, about 16 of us. In a hurry: this recital has been the usual damn nuisance, especially as Rosamond lives in the same house, and the organising secretary seems a very expensive nitwit. And I've been to tea with Sir Frederick Pollock, now aged about 90, and to a sherry party at the Rothensteins, and again promised to sit for a portrait. In fact, almost a whirl.

The conversazione took place on a fine evening early in May 1937, 'Under the patronage of Their Royal Highnesses the Duke and Duchess of Kent'. Princess Marina of Greece had married the Duke of Kent in Westminster Abbey in 1934, and their wedding had caused a happy stir throughout the British Isles. That May evening the Duchess of Kent looked very young and supremely elegant in diaphanous brown chiffon. She certainly did not require the sumptuousness of Londonderry House to enhance her beauty, but it was an effective setting.

Adila Fachiri and Jelly d'Aranyi, two Hungarian sisters, both violinists, opened the concert and contributed several items; Leonie Zifado sang Spanish songs, and a small orchestra of ten instrumentalists, all women with names well known in London society played Bach's Concerto in D Minor. At intervals Helen read her own unpublished poem *New York* and two of her own translations from the Latin; first 'Earth for the Sun her Lover', an exquisite lyric from Milton's '*In Adventum Verum*', and, to end the concert '*Veni Sancto Spiritus*' by Stephen Langton, Archbishop of Canterbury and the first signatory of Magna Carta.

No doubt the Over Thirty Association benefited financially

from this charity performance, but the evening belonged to Helen.

About this time Helen received an invitation which caused her excited pleasure and some trepidation: it came from 10 Downing Street.

Dear Miss Waddell,

Queen Mary is lunching with us on April 15th and she wants to meet you and we want you to meet her. Will you be with us at 1.20?

Yours sincerely,

Lucy Baldwin.

Before the great day arrived Helen told a friend that:

In spite of all Irish and republican sentiments, I am a little rattled by the prospect of tomorrow – lunch at the Baldwins to meet Queen Mary herself – and at Mary's own wish. I can only imagine that *The Desert Fathers* reached her just in her anguish about the little King, and that's why she wants me to be brought. But I was terribly touched.

This is how she described the event to Meg:

Darling, I've just come back from 10 Downing Street – a big lunch party – about eighteen – I between James Barrie and Montagu Norman. And Queen Mary was enchanting. She shook hands and we curtseyed all round to begin with, and then at coffee-time each lady was led by Mrs. S.B. to the Queen's sofa, and had a little chat. I went to the lunch nearly paralysed with funk, not so much of Mary, but all the gallery: only as usual, once the water breaks over your head, it all seems quite normal. Mary was exactly like her pictures, but she suddenly breaks down and laughs and laughs – in the most enchanting way, as if she was fifteen. She asked me if I could work in London – and how it was I began doing medieval things – and how I came to Latin. And I asked her if she read it – and she began with her little deep chuckle and said: '*Mensa*, *mensa*, *mensam*', and then she stuck. But she said that she always hankered above all to be able to read the Latin on old things – epitaphs, tomb-stones and inscriptions.

I'd just begun to feel that there was nothing you couldn't say to Mary, when Philip Sassoon was brought up, because he had to get back to the House, and I reluctantly parted. And after that it was one man after another. I hated Montagu Norman – but Lord Lothian was there, and we talked enormously – he adored *Abelard*. In fact I could hear him talking about it at lunch to some of the dowagers. It was funny going up the red carpet to No. 10 Downing Street, and coming away seeing all the cameras levelled. Mrs. S.B. was a wonderful hostess – introduced everybody as if it were Magherally. And S.B. and I as usual conducted an intense flirtation in five minutes and parted with grief. I spent the morning at the British Museum so as to steady my panic, and returned to it: I only wore my smart moss-green frock, and the green amber beads, and a new pair of grey gauntlet gloves, and a little grey hat *exactly* like the last one – but clean, and my grey fox fur, and I really looked quite nice. Tell Daddy from me that I feel about him and Magherally as I do about S.B. and the Cabinet – and told him so today – 'Wherever the MacGregor sits, will be the head of the table.'

CHAPTER XV

War on the Horizon

Helen refused the pleadings of relatives and friends to leave London: instead she lived on in her own house at Primrose Hill throughout the six years of War – and gradually paid the cost, which increased each year.

Her letters describe her life and her reactions: her spirit is revealed in the poems she wrote during the war. Some are original creations out of her own sensitive emotions, some are translations from poets who wrote in Latin in the medieval era she loved, or in earlier times.

The studio she had rented temporarily for the sake of peace from distractions and interferences of domesticity, had to be relinquished when she took up the post of assistant-editor to F. A. Voigt, the editor of the magazine *The Nineteenth Century*, which was published from the offices of Constable & Co.

Otto Kyllmann, who still had a flat in her house, and F. A. Voigt for whom she worked, were both elderly men, both passionately pro-British in spite of German extraction, German heredity and German characteristics. Both were absorbed, to the point of obsession, in European politics and the issues and strategies of the war. They were fundamentally kind men in intention, but temperamentally egotistic and demanding in practice, often ineffective and sometimes blinkered. O.K. was an admiring friend of Lord Vansittart, and F.A.V. had once been Vansittart's secretary.

Inadequate domestic help certainly had a large share in Helen's difficulties – on which she laid too much stress in her letters and conversation. Her nerves were more deeply frayed by the frustration of original creative work, in which she could lose herself and gain spiritual renewal, than by the noise of guns and the disasters of air raids.

For Helen – as for so many others – the war really began in 1938, the year of Munich: nevertheless friends and social occasions loom large in her correspondence in the first half of that year. For instance in the spring there is a note from Stanley Baldwin:

My dear Helen,

For these three months I have got myself once more immersed and I have a number of little functions and speeches ahead and a curiously assorted lot of people who oddly enough want to come and talk to me.

Which makes it the more needful that I should keep sane. To that end you can contribute. Come and keep me company on Sunday morning at 9.15 – breakfast.

I shall have had a long day on Saturday receiving a presentation in Worcester, and you would be peculiarly welcome the next morning!

Don't refuse because the next four Sundays I am out of London (three of 'em speeches).

Yours ever

S.B.

Don't bother to write: telephone.

Then a letter to Meg after a weekend in the Isle of Wight:

Ventnor enchanting, and I suddenly felt I could write again. Queer how being alone always rouses that silent creative toad in me that goes under a stone when I am enjoying myself with other people or being domestic. Lunching tomorrow at the Astors to meet the Shaws and Tom Jones.

But as the summer faded out, uncertainty and dread of the future deepened. The shadow of war became tangible at Munich in September, and no one, optimist or pessimist, could escape the apprehensive atmosphere that hung over the western world. Helen reacted as always when upset:

> My darlings, if only I were at Kilmacrew. Our collapse this morning to Germany has poisoned me body and spirit. I occupied myself for ten minutes composing a letter to *The Times*. . . . They'll not put it in, but it relieves my feeling. O.K. is very anxious that *The Times* should at least have to read it.
>
> But now the B.B.C. demand the MS of the schools broadcast this week for their various fiddling purposes.

Then a few days later she lets off steam to a friend about the reception of the broadcast:

> I sent in the B.B.C. broadcast, rather a nice one, written with Europe at the guillotine. They've just replied asking will I alter this and cut that, and leave out Goldsmith as children will never have heard of him, and they would like someone else to read the verse – to break up the monotony for the children, and when could I come for rehearsal, etc. So I sent them a nice note this morning offering them the MS to do what they liked with, omitting my name except as supplying some of the material, as I have no more time or energy to spend on it. They mean well, but they can leave nothing alone, and I can't be bothered with them. . . . I so hate the B.B.C. atmosphere anyhow, that I am glad of the chance to escape. And O.K. heartily approves. They've ruined quite enough of my time and spoiled any chance of finishing 'John of Salisbury'. . . . And now, darling, that has done me good, and none of this got into my letter – except that I suggested they omit the names of Virgil and the men which occur in one of the lustier poems.

When Czechoslovakia fell apart under Hitler's pressure in March 1939, only the date of the outbreak of war remained uncertain, and apprehension changed into an urgent speeding-up of practical preparedness.

While waiting for Hitler's speech to the Reichstag in reply to an appeal from President Roosevelt for a delay before a declaration of war, Helen wrote an anguished poem which she sent to her sister with a covering note:

> My darling, you and I were in the same mood, thinking the same things. It has turned colder now, but for two days when the world seemed to be holding its breath, I could not go into the garden without a kind of trance of deep strong delight. The pear was out and the cherry, and the light was still gold as if June were in the heart of April. And I began to write a thing in my head – not finished yet and very poor, but it will show you what was in my mind.

Earth said to Death,
Give these a little breath.
Give them eight days.
Eight days to feel the sun,
To see the limes in leaf.
Eight days:
Before the white flies come
Crawling upon the ceiling of the world.
Myself, I ask no stay,
Mine is a longer day,
But theirs is brief.

Who rives me, does but plough my field for grain,
But these, I cannot make them live again.

  Give me eight days,
And I will pour the silence of June
  Into this April noon.
  Wine of October in the vine still curled,
  Then let you come.
Darkness shall find their sleeping undismayed.
  Who shall make them afraid
  Who saw eternity
In the brief compass of an April day?

Helen sent a copy of this poem to a friend with a letter:

> I send you a thing I wrote during the strange trance of summer that came about April 20, before the Reichstag speech. I didn't publish it, for once it was written I felt that visionary bully had no right to hold the world to ransom, and I wouldn't admit the effect he had had on me for a day or two. But it had a wide application that speech on the 28th, and I'd like you to see it.
>
> I've tried to persuade O.K. that if the war comes, he will close C. & Co. for two months; and perhaps he will, but if he stays here so will I. One suffers more deaths away from people one cares for, than in the Hell's broth with them.
>
> Great cheerfulness on the arrival of my brother (Sam Waddell) to watch rehearsals of his play 'Bridgehead' at the Westminster (all notices good). It was lovely having Meg – a really stronger Meg this time. Robert Donat and his wife were here for a beer and kipper and sausage supper after the first night of 'Bridgehead' – almost to a day the anniversary of the absurd party after the first night of my own play in 1935. And all the evening Meg and I were haunted by Basil. . . . Alas, Wilfred Lawson has to go to America – a Hollywood contract – for the last week of the play.

Poetry remained Helen's refuge, almost a medieval sanctuary, throughout the war. Several of her original and many of her translated verses saw daylight in *The Times*, *The Manchester Guardian*, *The Nineteenth Century*, or in quotations on the radio, but as yet they have not been published in book form.

Few adults who lived through August 1939 will forget the suspense day after day as they waited for the declaration of war. Mollie Martin, Helen's niece, had come to London to work and to live in the Primrose Hill house. 'Every Sunday,' wrote her aunt, 'we go to Lewes, and I believe it does us all the good in the world. I feel in the morning as if I'd gladly never see a golf club again, but once up on those amazing downs all the fatigue goes and you come home a changed animal. Mollie says so too, and dear O.K. is incredibly fit and cheery.'

Only at the very end of August, after the German–Soviet pact, did her tone change:

> Darling, it just hasn't been possible to write. London is a very queer place these days, and one alternates between a desperate hope that England will save her honour, and depression. O.K. plays bridge with frightful intensity, but is now, thanks to our stiffer back, in a kind of quiet exaltation. And Roosevelt's message this morning makes everyone hope that Hitler will think twice. Myself I doubt. He has the mind of the frog that blew itself up to be like the bull, and I wish the explosion would come in Germany before he blows a lot of nice people up with him.
>
> Did I tell you that Hugh Verrall and I have moved the rockery against the kitchen window? It makes a marvellous dugout now.
>
> O.K. firmly convinced that Hitler is breaking up and vows that there won't be a war. . . . What bewilders us all is to know why he didn't march when the world stood on its head at the German–Soviet pact, a lightning stroke in his usual histrionic fashion. I am still blinking. But the magnificent indifference of the English reaction has brought me wholly in love with that race: and I forgive *The Times* all its sins for a single phrase even on the final thunderstruck morning: 'If Moscow confirms what the Berlin Press claims, one can only say that Soviet tactics are a little odd.' A little odd!
>
> I'll be helping at Constable's, but first job is to take parties of Mothers and Infants-in-arms from the East End down to the country. I have an armlet, and when I wear it I shall have all the feelings of an officer in uniform. I ought to get a gas mask, and instead I stand and think how to make a little run for hens at the foot of the garden. Don't be vexed if I try to carry on with the minimum of outside help. I *do* want the house to myself, and not to be driven from it by talkative females, all

interfering with one's mental processes. Let the place go dirty. Half of it is unused even now anyhow.

Oh Meg darling, if you could come over and see me, for in the present régime I am pretty well tied down here. That is the one snag. And anyhow I want you to add London in war-time to your experience. You that are so sensitive to all the movements of history should not lose this major one.

The weather since our return has been dead and sodden, not a gleam or breath. I'm working hard – some lovely stuff I finished today from Boethius (6th century):

'O Father, give the spirit power to climb
To Thy high throne,
In the fountain of all good to be purified,
To find Thy light, and fix on Thee its gaze.
Thrust back the mists of the earth, the weight of the clod,
Shine forth in splendour, Thou that art calm weather,
And quiet resting-place for faithful souls.
To see Thee is the end and the beginning,
Thou carriest us, and Thou dost go before.
Thou art the journey, and the journey's end.'

CHAPTER XVI

The Fact of War

At 11 o'clock on the morning of Sunday, September 3rd 1939, war became an ineluctable fact, thrilling to some, appalling to others, fateful to all.

The circumstances that precluded all chances of Helen giving any more books to the world are too vividly apparent in her letters to need any word of explanation. The selection from so much material has been governed hopefully by the intention to let her paint in her own words a picture not only of the war, but of her literary frustrations and reactions, and also the reactions of those she loved, and with whom she lived, thought, worked and suffered. The magic of the spiritual radiation from her personality breathed consolation and hope throughout.

Helen's first letter to Meg actually has a full date – Monday September 4th 1939 – which shows it was a unique day in her mind.

> And meantime there is a new way of living for us two, in one night. I shan't talk of the possibilities, or of the boys [her three nephews]. I have had moments when I think anything would have been better than to keep our word, because of the price. But they are only a flash of sudden anguish and fear. The boys themselves would have it this way. I think far more than in 1914, people feel that they are fighting 'principalities and powers and the rulers of darkness'.
>
> As for this small section of your family – O.K. and Mollie and me – we've never been so fond of each other or so in a way lighthearted. Mollie woke me last night about 3 a.m. to say the hooters were blowing for a raid. O.K. was strolling about in his

dressing gown, and Rosamond, and the little Quaker ladies sitting side by side like two mice on the kitchen divan. It all seemed quite ordinary and yet foolish and strange. So I put on the kettle to make tea, and suddenly O.K. yawned and said: 'Well, if you'll excuse me, I'm going back to bed' – and went upstairs again. It was the one absolute gesture – I feel it has given the tuning-fork note for all future raids. And sure enough, in a few minutes came the All Clear.

A week or two later she tells Meg:

It's about 10.30 p.m. and O.K. gone to bed, and Mollie not yet home from A.R.P. duty, which keeps her at Mitcham every Tuesday night – just sitting in the Town Hall waiting for air alarms.

George* did get up to see us and hopes to more often, because they've sent a new major. Bunt, George's friend, has just sent me a hopeful letter about being in town next weekend. He is in the Canadian Air Force down on Salisbury Plain, so I've told him that this is his home for all purposes. John Mulligan is in the R.A.M.C. and I'm expecting him any time. In short, I always felt the house might become a kind of depôt for the young of His Majesty's Forces, and it looks like it. O.K. is frightfully pleased it should be.

These are queer days and Finland doesn't bear thinking of. I've stopped talking to Rosamond about politics or the war, for her attachment to Russia last time we spoke beats any ignorant Catholic to the Pope. It's an odd sidelight on the absolute necessity to the human mind of some kind of religion based on a personal God – and these idiot Communists worship that Mongolian-countenanced Stalin as no Catholic ever worshipped the Pope. I had hoped that the debunking of Russia would give English Communism an independent one – red, bloody, revolution chance: but they still go tagging after the cat's meat man. . . . I'm very sleepy today for I was doing an all-day job yesterday on the proofs of Villard's articles in the *Daily Tele-*

*George Martin, Meg's youngest son.

graph. This new world is very like the old, except that everybody is much nicer. Mrs. McLeod refuses any evenings off and Hugh Verrall has been invaluable, for with me being away all day, he has done a lot of window-dressing himself.

Rosamond is now at G.H.Q. of the Wrens at Kingsway, so she is terribly happy. I shan't have so much to do for the XIXTH in a few days, for Alec will be passing his A.R.P. exams, and, though on regular night duty till morning, can come in next week about two in the afternoon. So I've moved my books into a funny little room at Constable's. Mr. Warner the caretaker has gone to his old job with the Navy, but Mrs. Warner refuses to budge from her eyrie at the top of the house. She respects me because I haven't run away. She and I are the only women left in Constable's. Michael Sadleir is down in the country getting in the harvest while he waits for his job with the Foreign Office, and Martha Smith is at the sea with her old mother. All the young men are gone, or waiting for their summons. O.K. is in marvellous spirits. The knowledge that we have let no one down is meat and drink to him. Last night Dreiser* asked us all to dinner. He'd just arrived from Barcelona. Voigt came too, and it was a tremendous evening of good talk. Arnold Wilson† is giving up the *Nineteenth Century* and Voigt is to be the new editor.

Helen paid a visit to Kilmacrew in October, and her reaction to the defeat of Poland is in the first letter to Meg after her return.

Darling, there is nothing to say – 'This is their hour and the power of darkness'. I sent that cable we talked of to Roosevelt on Saturday night: 'The horn in Roncevalles has blown again. Is the world deaf? Must Poland die in vain?' I must not go on about it.

I have never had such a welcome home. Mollie and O.K.

*American author and speaker.

†Arnold Wilson (1884–1940), held Fascist views before the war: disillusioned in 1939, enlisted in R.A.F. and was killed flying in 1940.

were both at the station, and we had an uproarious lunch at the Escargot, and came back to find the house just stacked with flowers. Everybody gapes at my improved appearance.

Both Helen and O.K. became involved at once in assistance to Polish refugees: that their friendship with Feliks Topolski, the Polish artist, began then is supported by a letter from him to Helen in which he refers to a dinner 'that you and O.K. gave to the officers of one of our submarines'.

Helen translated *The White Eagle*, a popular, ultra-patriotic Polish ballad into English. When asked how she could translate from a language of which she did not understand a word, her reply was that she caught the rhythm when they sang it and someone told her the approximate meaning.

In December she mentions 'a marvellous dinner at Palmstierna's, and Sir Hubert Gough (of the Fifth Army) was there, such an enchanting little man. And Mollie enjoyed it enormously. It was fun being out to dinner again, for in this black-out one goes nowhere.'

The first Christmas of the war was greeted with almost frenetic efforts to ignore or disguise realities: the holiday came in the period known as 'the phoney war', and the atmosphere had to include peace and pleasure, an excuse in some cases valid, for the 'children's sake'.

Helen was deeply disappointed by O.K.'s refusal to go to Kilmacrew and writes:

Meg darling, I know you will understand about Christmas. It isn't the journey in winter: it's that he isn't budging from Constable's till Saturday evening, and is determined to be in the office by himself on Tuesday morning. It's this marvellous little book by Villard: it only comes out on the 15th, and he thinks it's going to be a real seller. . . . He is absolutely on his toes about it, and I don't like to leave him to have Christmas all alone, but O my dear, when are we going to see each other? O.K. says he thinks Easter would be possible for him, and I'll try to squeak over after New Year. Somehow life is different since the war: it's as if one were in so deep and swift a river that one's own affairs are only a small bent twig making a brief eddy that is wiped out in a moment.

Nothing 'phoney' was left about the war when, in April 1940, Hitler sent his troops into Norway and into France in the same month. During Germany's conquest of France, Helen looked again to her usual source of consolation:

I have been so haunted by France that I went back to Virgil, the fall of Troy, and all the old Fifth Column business of the Trojan Horse, and the tearful refugee who was the traitor. It might be yesterday.

This will be a poor letter, for there is thunder about. The birds very quiet and even London, and one is heavy and restless – you know the feeling. But I must just hold your hand for a minute. I keep reading about the danger to Ireland, and my inside turns over thinking of you and Daddy and Kilmacrew. But this is cowardly.

I can't think about France. My heart cracks. Instead I imagine consternation in the old kitchen over 2 oz. ration of tea. Thank heaven Daddy is now fond of coffee.

I enclose Michael's letter on France, written before she sank into this strange darkness. I still feel as if one of us were dead – and the funeral not yet over. It is so strange and lonely a thing to have one's mind go as usual joyfully and confidently across the Channel, and suddenly it begins groping in a cold impalpable mist.

Letter from Michael Sadleir, dated June 14th 1940.
My dear Helen,

I ought to have written you an answer to your lovely letter about my novel (*Fanny by Gaslight*), but there seemed no need to thank you for saying thank you, and I just treasured the letter and said nothing. Now, however, as one lover of France to another, in this hideous moment of France's agony, I feel I must send a few words if only to create a fragile, useless, but desperately sincere little barricade against the onrush of barbarism.

When I read of fighting at Senlis, I feel that I am watching a buck-nigger snapping a girl's wrist across, or a race-course gang making a latrine of Vézelay. Senlis – already brutalised in 1914 and since restored to a wistful dignity, too certain of its tradition to mind having a few ruins, has had to suffer all over again. And within an hour they have been at Ermenonville and Montefontaine.

In a queer sort of way I feel almost glad that 'Fanny's' material prospects are buried under the débris of the country which gave her peace at last. Somehow the death of the only chance of a big sale I shall ever have seems like a sort of contribution to the lament for France, which screams silently in my throat all day. If only it could have been turned into cash first and the cash used to succour those grand indifferent civilised people. Now there is little cash and succour is almost too late.

They cannot finally conquer the spirit of civilisation, but they can scar and terrify it. The vision of any one of those little gentle kindly towns smashed and straddled by a mechanical force which means not one damn thing in comparison with the untidy 'place' in front of the hideous Mairie, or the racks of shoddy gay clothing outside the Dames de France, makes one physically sick – me, at any rate.

And you too, I am sure. That is why I wrote like this. Perhaps you, who can do it so wonderfully, will write something about Auxerre and Semur, about Cahors and Rodez, about a hundred other corners of the real France. Salute them, and spit on Le Touquet and the Riviera de luxe, and Biarritz where the playboys of the world which has destroyed itself (and us with it) insulted France and betrayed their order.

Incessantly the faces of Bonnet and Chamberlain and Hoare – loops and strings of faces which controlled power and policy over our stupid lazy heads – hang between the mind's eye and the grey and shabby but always understanding and self-respecting townships of the Île de France. There nothing matters except a human being be a human being, and that life should have balance and suavity. But the faces were turned away and did not care. God grant they care before they are done.

Yours

MICHAEL

To Monica Blackett she wrote more practically early in July, and enclosed a copy of the poem on Rome:

I am hearty, and best of all I've begun – out of my anguish, I think – to work again. The Rome poem may be in *The Times* one of these days, 'For Vilipuri, Cracow, Prague': if not I'll send it to the *Observer*. I've promised (having lunched with Mary Ogilvie) to let her husband see 'Hitler Speaks', with a view to my reading it at the B.B.C.

The day of the peace terms I grieved as I had done for Basil – and in the same quality – as if strength, valiancy, courage, had suddenly gone into the depths – but in certain hope of a glorious resurrection.

My love always,

HELEN

For Vilipuri, Cracow, Prague

(Translated from a fragment written by Alcuin during the occupation of Rome by the Lombards).

By these, by these same chains, O Rome,
Thou art more strong.
Thy faith more absolute
Against the wrong.
For ever art thou free; what bonds avail
When He hath touched them, who absolveth all?
That heart unconquered and these solemn walls
Shall stand, shaken it may be, not destroyed,
By any trampling of the hosts of hate.
The road is closed to war, whose gate
Stands open to the stars.

Helen Waddell

The start of frequent air raids in 1940, and the urgent offers of hospitality from friends or relations in Canada or the U.S.A. made a number of anxious parents send their small children – sometimes with their mothers or nurses – to safety in North America. Helen's friends, Charles Morgan the novelist and his wife, were one such case, and in August she tells Meg about them:

> Hilda Morgan and the two children left for America in the middle of the week. Charles felt they ought to go, and O.K. and I went to say goodbye on Monday. Charles very wretched at it but convinced it must be, and wants to come to us a lot. He came to dinner last night, and he was so dear. Hilda says he just adores O.K. He was broadcasting 'And So to Bed' at midnight, and quoting two of my *Lyrics* – 'Love, let us live as we have lived, Nor lose the little names that were the first night's grace'. He told Hilda to listen in at sea.
>
> Darling, don't worry your darling head about us for one moment. We were never better or fitter or cheerier, and when the air raid sirens sound we yawn and stay in bed, for the guns being at our elbow we know it would be time enough to stir when we hear them go. They've never gone yet.

And to Monica Blackett:

> I'm working at Constable's now. Hugh Verrall here for a few weeks: O.K. overjoyed to have a young man in this house in case of emergency. In spite of raids increasing, I am working and O.K. deeply happy in himself and very busy, for the staff depletes almost daily.
>
> Two things of Alcuin I have been working on recently will be lyric but some prose: 'O King of Glory and Lord of valours, our warrior and our peace'. And this: 'The world is full of many griefs, and there is no comfort but in this, the mercy of God and the faith of our friends'. That says all that can be said.

But by the first week in September Helen was writing:

One grand night our guns on Primrose Hill spoke out, and very loud they were. It really was magnificent, and O.K.'s face lit up with delight. He said: 'Nothing more cheers me than the Roar of the Angry Lions!' (You know his touch of capitals). Sometimes we all three go up to O.K.'s bathroom window with all lights extinguished, and sit in a row as in the Dress Circle, seeing the amazing sky, with the great searchlights wheeling and turning and locking, then suddenly converging; and then the shells bursting round that spot – far off intolerably bright small fires, not shooting stars, because they fall in a stream of light, but a single flaring star that blazes one second and then goes out.

Mollie saw a glorious dogfight yesterday at Mitcham. She was at the vicarage and a row started. She and the vicar's wife dashed to the door, and for about ten minutes saw the sight of their lives. The sky looked like a flight of rooks, splitting and diving, and banging and dancing, and they watched and cheered till it seemed better to take cover. You see, over London they have to fly so high that you can hardly see anything, only now and then a small glint of silver like the scale of a sardine up in the blue, but beyond the balloon barrage they come down and the fun begins. . . . I have dislodged the little Quaker ladies into the garden room, for I have joined the 'Housewives Service', which means that one must be able to hear the doorbell at night, and have a warm place to bring shivering evacuated people into.

In October Helen describes a cottage she rented at Lewes:

You see, we all badly want weekends out of London, but it does come expensive. . . . One Sunday afternoon we saw it. And I knew my Fate. You go up the hill to Lewes Castle, there the road dips to the other side past two brick houses. Then there is a high garden wall with a door in it. And inside is a small cottage built like a lean-to against one of the little houses, with small latticed windows and oak beams and a floor of red brick. There is a very old apple tree in the middle of the garden, and you walk past it, and realise that you are on the castle wall. But, oh my darling, when one goes there at sunset, hanging as it does like a cell above the world, with the strange haze turning golden, you feel you have come to a holy place.

But there's a strange grief with it all, for the one person who would have loved it most is dead. Hugh Verrall, dear Hugh, in an accident to an express train near Wembley. An overloaded barrow running onto the line. I know it is better for him, but he enjoyed so many things, and with all his preposterous ways was so dear and gentle and friendly. And always that glancing genius in sudden shafts of light. (I have a lot of his pictures). We knew that he was 'seriously injured' on Monday, and when O.K. came down he said he had died shortly after. O.K. is marvellous. They are already putting in the windows, and the office is running as usual.*

Helen also sends a letter to Meg full of news of the Blitz:

It is sad to reflect that it is only five days since I wrote to you, for in between one's life seems to have had such odd experiences. . . . Our disturbance began on Saturday afternoon. I was in a great gale of work, in fact I've collected most of the stuff, and given O.K. roughly the paging. But rooting through my papers I came on a dozen lines I hadn't seen since I was collecting stuff for *The Wandering Scholars*. It's ninth century, a lament for an abbess – I think she was another Héloise – and I began translating:

> 'Thou art come safe to port,
>   I still at sea.
> The light is on thy head,
>   Darkness in me.
> Pluck thou in heaven's fields
>   Violet and rose,
> While I strew flowers that will thy vigil keep

*Bombs fell on Constable's offices in Orange Street several times, and windows were frequently blown out by blast.

Where thou dost sleep
Love, in thy last repose.'

It was one of those days rich with melody chanting in one's head, and I was drunk with the stuff I was doing. (I'd told the family to lunch out for I wanted to work.) But about five I came down and just filled the teapot when a roar of such violence hit my ears that I made one leap for the grotto, and Toty streaked past me for the garden with ears back and tail out. The whole house shuddered and groaned, and from where I sat I saw red flashes, like pointed tongues of flame stabbing the old kitchen; I could see them through the door. Then the tempo got faster, and five bangs went off one after another, and all the while these strange tongues of flame stabbing into the kitchen. . . . That was the overture to what has been happening since. . . . You can imagine the anguish of my dear family when they saw as they walked that our Primrose Hill gun was going and Helen alone at 32. They dashed into Muriel Byrne's to telephone to me and I implored them to stay there and not attempt to come home till things quietened down. After a time kind Muriel Byrne drove them back in her car, and they all came in and had sherry in the grotto, and they thought my poem the loveliest thing I had ever done. (I forgot to tell you that all the time I was working out, 'Love, on thy last repose', there were interludes like 'Love on thy (crump) last repose' (crump, crump), but dull cosy crumps that only sounded like distant tom-toms, menacing, but good for poetry. Poor Toty had dashed in from the garden at the second gun, but saw me in the grotto and was just coming to my blandishing when the five-fold bang went off and the red glare came in, and the poor fellow streaked upstairs, and was found hours after very bundled and solemn under the sideboard, a very good choice for air-raid shelter. Since then the nights have been middling noisy.

CHAPTER XVII

Pressures of War

By 1941 every Government in the world was involved in the Second World War, even if not as a direct combatant. Such a vast upheaval dislocated the routine affairs of mankind everywhere. Yet the pen still remained a powerful weapon in the days when the sword claimed indisputable superiority.

However, as Helen said herself, she was not a 'political animal'. She was profoundly wearied by her work on the *Nineteenth Century*. A desire to help out, however strong, is no substitute for finding satisfaction in the work itself, and her employers, O.K. and F. A. Voigt, had no interest beyond the politics of the war in Europe. They remained their egotistic selves, inside and outside their offices, and Helen accepted their one-track minds and conversation and was inevitably victimised.

Her relations at Kilmacrew played an increasingly important part in her life; Meg as her *alter ego*, and Mollie who came to London and lived in her aunt's house while commuting to her own work in Mitcham and Chelsea.

Helen, in spite of the unpredictable comings and goings of her domestic helpers, always kept open house for her nephews and any friends of theirs in H.M. Forces. By 1941 Jack Martin was in the Rhodesian Air Force; Charles and George were both engineers, the former in the R.N.V.R. and the latter in the R.E. Jack was married with two children, Charles was unmarried, and George married two days before he was posted to Tobruk.

O.K. delighted in uniforms and marching feet, and his addiction to meals in small restaurants was a domestic asset to Helen in the days of rationing and food shortages. Social gatherings were pleasures of the past, but Lord and Lady Astor still managed to entertain at Cliveden. Helen's comments on her first visit are brief and unembroidered: 'The lunch at Lady Astor's was interesting, but I don't like her. She is shrill and combative, and kicked off by a diatribe against the Jews. I fought her tooth and nail, with the result that she was all over me and very anxious to have me again, but I came home with depression on me.' Then, after a further visit in July, another brief comment: 'I was at Cliveden for Wednesday night, but tale too long to tell. Nancy kept me up till two; came to my room to talk. If you can imagine a fierce 'Mammy B'* with the lovely spontaneity that redeems all faults. I've sworn to go back, but was firm about not going there to finish my book.'

The mixture of air raids and parties was not exactly a happy one as Helen shows:

> Life has been cheerful in spite of everything. O.K. and I gave the Voigts a birthday party, and had Dulanty and Topolski – the Polish artist who did Churchill that O.K. was going to send to you. I wonder did he? Alas, dear Topsy as we call him, was caught in Saturday's blitz, sketching in the light of the fires, and is now in the Middlesex Hospital rather bashed and bruised, but nothing serious, and already sketching his nurses.
>
> Poor old Constable's got another biff soon after Easter; not a direct hit but H.E. on the same spot as before on the ruins of Garlands Hotel, and all our windows that had been carefully filled up by the Army and Navy Stores are gaping again and dust and rubbish everywhere. But dear O.K. is marvellous well, thinner, but just the old soldier.

The cottage that Helen found at Lewes was declared 'in a Defence Area' and had to be abandoned, a great disappointment. Helen had become conscious of the censor's blue pencil, so only mentions it indirectly:

> We had a lovely Easter at the little house, and said goodbye to it. I have not yet moved the furniture, for I've been wondering

*A talkative nurse, a friend of the Martin family.

if we couldn't find some labourer's cottage near a links in a not defence area, and then the one move would do. For now that Mollie is such a good golfer she adores it, and it is really rather good to get a complete change and wake up in a different place.

A little later, probably early in May 1941, during the heaviest raids on the large and crowded cities of the British Isles, including a savage one on Belfast:

> My dear, my dear, Heaven bless you for that telegram. When the paper said 'All Ulster' my heart said 'Kilmacrew', and Daddy's lamp suddenly became a bale fire. Yet I felt quite irrationally, that you were safe, all of you: just as I think you must feel it about us: only the reassurance of that wire was blessed. I am longing, we all are, to hear if they came near you. How long it seems since the little lambs mewed among the high trees in the orchard: and last year, when all the chickens took cover.

In 1941 the Germans miscalculated the cost in men and machines of sustaining heavy air raids, and over-estimated their effect on the morale of the people of Britain. Gradually, the raids petered out. Moreover, after Hitler's attack on the U.S.S.R., the Luftwaffe had its hands full elsewhere.

Meanwhile, Helen's efforts to cope with work for Constable and assist Voigt gave her less and less time to call her soul her own to translate the Latin poems of medieval and earlier days. At intervals, usually after some particular episode in the war, verses of hers appeared in *The Times* or *The Nineteenth Century* or *The Manchester Guardian*. She was approached more than once to contribute to books brought out in aid of some wartime charity. She never refused, but as early as June 1941, she complains to Meg:

> Alas, I've promised to do something for one of these war books – this time for Greek famine relief. God help them, but it always sends the end of my own book one step further back. I

wonder is it a mistake to be completely catholic in liking? In fancy in Japan, then France, and the downs at Savernake. But not completely: it's a queer thing that mountains you only knew from 1920 on (except to look at from a distance) are still 'the fountain light of all our day. Are still the master-light of all our seeing'. That, and Chartres. But I suppose if one's people for almost three hundred years have lived in sight of the Mournes, they are in our blood. . . .

Did I tell you that the diplomatic correspondent of *The Times* told Voigt that he reads a piece of *Abelard* when he feels he is losing his grip of any reality? I imagine 'diplomatics' must seem more unreal than anything one has to handle. I don't know if I sent you this fragment from Alciun:

'Too wide the earth: mine eyes no more behold him.
Love weeps for absent love; my friend is gone.
Rare, rare in men the faith that can unite them.
Cry to the world: thy heart is still alone.'

P.S. I enclose a letter from Dr. Dwelly, the Dean of Liverpool, about a new version of my '*How mighty are the Sabbaths*' and rough draft of my reply. . . . It was very sweet of him: but I won't have a chorus. . . . When I come you will be able to play me Gustav Holst's setting. . . . The tune the Dean wants is the same as 'Glory, laud and honour'.

And a draft of Helen's reply to the Dean:

It is far less popular – even in J. M. Neale's version – than those on a similar theme by Bernard of Morlaix: more rugged and exciting. *Jerusalem the Golden* has all the summer Sundays of one's childhood in it; but here there is the whiteness of eternity. For this reason to divide it into single verse and chorus is, I think, to do it wrong, being so majestical. Moreover the chorus dwells on what is the least part of Abelard's version – the courts, the rest, the refreshing – and exaggerates what is the worst fault of my own translation – the transposing of '*Quis rex quae curia*' as 'But of the courts of heaven and Him who is the king'. I am still working on a version that will correct it. If any one verse seems the theme, it is I think, the ultimate mystical experience, in words of one syllable – 'When God shall be all in all' – (*Cum erit omnia Deus in omnibus*). It is echoed again in the close.

It is presumption in a translator to speak with such positive conviction. Yet this took weeks of thinking and of experiments: and in those weeks I began to realise how close-knit is the thought, and with what certainty it moves to its consummation. The middle verse is the turning-point: it abandons paradise for the soul still in exile but with its face set to Jerusalem: and it must always be the middle verse, deep as is the temptation to bring it near the end. The earlier verses are impersonal, if indeed the deep amazing ecstasy can be described as impersonal: but after the '*nostrum est*' the thing is a pilgrims' chorus that has the weariness of exile in it, until it rings out into the final Jubilate – that angels sing with men. The last verse is not, I think, essential: Abelard ended almost every hymn he wrote with something like it.

After the fall of France Helen had been quickly in touch with the headquarters of the Free French in London, and soon there are references in her letters to a Frenchman whom she knew as 'Jacques'. She translated his articles for the *Nineteenth Century*, and in 1941 O.K. published them in a small book entitled *A French Soldier Speaks*. In a letter to Meg she refers to Jacques as a guest at a lunch party given by Rosamond Tweedy:

The party is to be at a Spanish restaurant, and I think Robert Donat is coming, and dear Dulanty, the High Commissioner, and Voigt and Jacques. His book we'll soon be reading. We have got a marvellous letter from America about his *Nineteenth Century* articles. I asked him would he like to dedicate the little book to his wife – the enchanting young wife, exactly like a French edition of you, and he was terribly touched. This is what he wrote – I told him we wouldn't translate it: 'A ma jeune femme qui, en France, m'attend, espère et prie'.

Helen and O.K. both sent copies of Jacques' book to friends they knew would be interested. Two letters of thanks reveal the impressive quality of it. Helen sent it to Meg with a covering letter.

> I've just had an amazing letter from dear old Stanley Baldwin. I hadn't written for years – you know how the war seems to silence one, but I did write suddenly the other day with a copy of 'A French Soldier Speaks'. . . . It's difficult on the XIXTH, for the paper shortage is so acute that we get cut down every month to fewer and fewer pages, and the articles accepted on the old valuation form longer and longer queues, and I spend hours cutting them to fit into less space without destroying their value or enraging the authors! But if I weren't doing this I'd feel I ought to go to munitions. This is a sad letter, but the truth is that I miss you and Kilmacrew so badly I almost try to forget.

(The lyric referred to in these letters from Stanley Baldwin and Max Beerbohm is 'Thou hast come safe to port'.)

From Stanley Baldwin.

Astley Hall,
Stourport-on-Severn.
18th June, 1941.

My dear Helen,

Since the death of Archimedes there has been no such instance of spirit subduing flesh as your working out your problems under a 4.7 barrage on Primrose Hill! It will be a magnificent passage, if given the right hand, when your life comes to be written. But I shan't be there to cheer.

During this long silence, bear me witness I never butted in. I have been too well-brought-up not to bow to the creative spirit, and when that spirit is silent, I am silent too. But it was a great moment when the spell was broken and I feel like Christian when he shed his burden.

I liked your book enormously: your French officer has a

beautiful mind. Could I have two or three copies to send to choice friends? *To be paid for, of course.*

More later, now the silence is broken and till then always

Your affec.

S.B.

From Max Beerbohm.

Abinger Manor Cottage,
Abinger Common,
Near Dorking.
June 26 1941

Our dearest Helen

Yes, by all means, let my such-as-it-is signature be tacked on to the admirable letter.

And ever so many thanks for sending us the French soldier's book. It is full of beauty and fine suffering and deep thought and astringent wit: a noble work. I hope it will have a wide circulation in Vichy. I made up a motto for 'ces gens là' the other day: Humilité, Servilité, Lavalité.

As for the translation, one would suppose the Irishwoman to be a Frenchman – were it not that no Frenchman has ever known one word of English.

And the lovely lyric, 1000 thanks for this too. But the portrait of the back of your head – where is that? It wasn't in your envelope.

We think and talk of you constantly, and long for another visit. Do, if you can in these harassing and hampered times, come.

Affectionately yours

MAX BEERBOHM

We are here in this hotel for a few days because our Austrian servant is having her holiday.

Helen also sent a copy to Marjorie Broughall, who had been her collaborator in *A Book of Medieval Latin for Schools*, and said: 'I'll soon be sending you a little book called 'A French Soldier

Speaks'. Jacques is like a Desert Father. His young wife is in Occupied France; no news since before the surrender last year. He chose to stay here: if he can't find her after the war is over he will take vows at Solesmes.'

Then on 26th August 1941 Helen wrote sadly to Meg:

I've just had a letter from a friend of Jacques, who had rung up the French H.Q. in London. Jacques had a fresh attack of pleurisy: on Friday he had, for the first time since he came to England, a letter from his young wife, saying that she was safe and well. Ten minutes after he had a heart attack and was dead in half an hour. I think he died in an ecstasy. One can see how it happened, the strain of pleurisy with only one lung (the other collapsed), and on the top of that the sudden snapping of the strain of anxiety and dread.

And yet I feel as if a deadweight had gone from me: it is like Lear – 'If she but live, It doth redeem all sorrow I have felt'.

Quite irrationally, I feel it is a good omen for our adored France. I had to let you know about him. I felt you knew him better than most people. It is idiotic to take things so to heart, but there was something about the funeral that broke me, and the whole grief of Europe was suddenly about one like a tide. In Alcuin's phrase – 'So vast the grief, so universal through the whole world'. And to know that Jacques went out in a sudden glory has transfigured it.

O.K. and I went down to Brookwood today to see him buried in the military cemetery there. It was a divine day with a soft wind, and it is a little wild just there, with trees and long grass and heather. We waited at the gate, and followed him – carried on the shoulders of French soldiers – and a handful of officers and two or three French women in black. His commander in France spoke over the grave, and then, with a last salute: 'Guy Robin – au revoir!'

Two days later Helen translated 'in a sudden pure relief of the spirit' Alcuin's dedication of an altar to St Michael the Archangel:

'O Michael, servant of the eternal King,
Standing upon the citadel of Heaven
Amid thy wingéd comrades, through the years
Of the abiding light, the kingdoms of white peace:
Protect this altar which we dedicate,
On earth, to thee.'

CHAPTER XVIII

Tragedy at Kilmacrew

Helen's genius for words was numbed, and she could find no consolation in them, when the hand of death touched her own two nephews within four months. Jack was killed in Rhodesia in November 1941, and George at Tobruk in March 1942 – both in accidents, not in battle.

When Jack's death was reported she caught the first boat to Belfast, but when George was killed only his young wife was allowed a permit. In the first case there was no need for letters; she and Meg were together. Perhaps, in the second case, she learned that sorrow can be too deep for words and silence deeper than tears.

To Meg. 32, Primrose Hill Road.
Wednesday, March 25th 1942.

My darling –

I can't write. George sits waiting on the settee in O.K.'s room, he walks into the Escargot, he watches O.K. make salad dressing, he stands in the hall getting into his overcoat, always that tilt at the corner of the eyelid, that far-back smiling. And if in every street in London I see him, what must it be for you at Kilmacrew?

My darlings, I could not do anything last night. The wire came about the same time as the last news about Jack. We were still at the office, just about to go home. I tried this morning, and wrote two things, which have gone to *The Times*, but I am so scared you will hate them. I seem to have no brain, as if it were anaemic; and maybe I should have waited. The notice is just as Daddy wished it.

Then I began writing a note to go under the 'Fallen Officers', but the only way I could do it to make it effective seemed to me to link him with his friend. . . . I feel so timid about it, but O.K. loves it, and Voigt who said that with one so young it seemed to him better to dwell rather on the two comrades-in-arms. And somehow I thought Willie McGrath had no one to speak for him. I saw in *The Times* of March 20th, just the bald – 'The Army. McGrath, Capt. W., D.S.O., R.E.' It didn't seem much after St. Valéry, and all the happy years with George. And I thought George would like it.

Darling, do forgive me if you think I have let you down in the notice. You see for one thing we knew so little of what he had done once he got East that there wasn't much I could say.

I tried to write of George and Jack together, but I couldn't, I just stuck. I think, if darling Mollie doesn't mind, that the book of translations will be dedicated to Jack and George, and the name of it will be the original name – 'And Honour Unforgotten'.

O my dear, I feel so far away. I wonder about Daddy. And if you were still in bed when this blow above the heart came on you. O live, my dearest, don't just drift out as it would be so easy to do. We need you so terribly. 'And having done all to stand'.

From *The Times*, March 1942.

Two young men, friends, have died in the Middle East within three weeks of each other – Major G. F. W. Martin, R.E. and Capt. W. McGrath, D.S.O., R.E. They entered Woolwich together, one from Down, one from Antrim; were at Cambridge together for a single, too brief year broken by the war. McGrath at 22 was sent to France to win the D.S.O. in the hell of St. Valéry; Martin, Acting-Captain at 21 was held, greatly chafing, at Derby to train older men in railway transport. In January 1941, he had his will and sailed for the Middle East; later McGrath followed him; now in death they are not divided.

HELEN WADDELL

The next day she writes again:

I cannot get over. O my love, I am thinking of you the whole day, but it's no good. I am absolutely all right, but I think the shock made me rather queer and gaspy yesterday at the office, and O.K. said I mustn't go till Dr. James had seen me. He came this morning and says it isn't my heart, but shock on top of anaemia, and that he utterly refuses to let me travel anywhere, let alone go to Ireland. . . . Oh dear, my heart is at Kilmacrew – I keep seeing all your faces.

But Helen never took orders from anyone when her emotions overwhelmed her, and as soon as the immediate shock was over she writes: 'I am sending this on anyhow, as letters are such a nuisance coming through the censorship. No news of the permit yet, and I am pawing the ground.' And a day or two later:

If only I could see you for one half hour, I think it would be easier. But as it is I seem to be stumbling along in a fog. It was so comforting to have Ethel* these two nights, the darling that she is. . . . I kind of collapsed the morning she was going away. . . .

I'll send you Barrington Ward's letter from *The Times*. . . . Something old Leonard said about his being thankful we hadn't had the blind dread of a casualty at Singapore suddenly shocked me into thankfulness when I thought of Alec's mother. O.K. did get through last week to the Air Ministry and was assured that Alec had been withdrawn from Singapore. . . . I wrote at once to his poor mother and she is in heaven.

Tell Daddy that what he wrote in the local paper was marvellous, I don't know how he did it. It was intimate, but so controlled and grave and wise, and with such recognition of other men's grief and loss.

Slowly the tone of Helen's letters lightens, after what perhaps may seem an extreme use of George's mother as an escape valve, but Meg's deep and gentle devotion saw only cause for

*Ethel: George's wife.

understanding and gratitude in her brilliant sister's outpourings. In April Helen begins at least to sublimate again:

> Dearest, that telegram about Tobruk stands on the mantelshelf always. It was the first thing that brought me out of the tunnel, into some kind of a human world, with light in it. For I had gone on and on – 'To what purpose is this waste?' And I suppose because it was Easter the half realisation came that it looks as if the world had always to be saved by someone else's pain and someone else's death – vicarious suffering whose efficacy we so heartily deny when we are young.
>
> But it was all no good. I wanted him to have had his hour – not only to have been busy with railways and transport. And then darling Ethel's telegram came, and the world went up in a glory. For Tobruk is one of the epic sieges, and George was there!
>
> The evening the telegrams came my head almost cracked with longing to be at Kilmacrew. One of the things I'll always remember with misery about these weeks is that I couldn't reach you, that for once you were in need of me, and I couldn't come. And it wasn't only that – it was just that I wanted you all, just for my own consoling.

Letters in this vein go on till the middle of June, when she starts dolefully, but ends on a practical note about her friends and about her work:

> It is strange how difficult I find it to write. I mean to, am anxious to, and when I come to it there is nothing worth saying. The queer thing is I miss George more than I did at Kilmacrew. For years I had never been there when he was there. . . . But Primrose Hill is full of him. . . . Jack belongs to Ormonde Terrace. All the absurd funny memories were Ormonde Terrace. . . . It doesn't get better with the passing of the weeks. It's, I imagine, like losing an arm. At first there's all the fuss, and necessity to be good and brave; and then you settle down to ordinary life, but with only one hand, that's all.

. . . Now that I have got some help I hope to get down to the lyrics. I know I must for I have a card stuck on my blotter with that translation beginning:

> 'The Word went forth,
> Yet from his Father never went away,
> Came to his walk on earth,
> And laboured till the twilight of his day.'

And the benediction it brings to me is so great every time a shuffle of papers brings it to light, that I think the book might have some consolation in it for the rest of us.

I went one afternoon to see Cornelia Sorabji (Indian lawyer) in her lovely old room at Lincoln's Inn, and Bruce Richmond's wife was there, a slow gentle woman with a twinkle. I'd brought Cornelia the thing I did on the Holy Ghost – 'The flowing, the giving, the light on our face', and Lady Richmond said: 'If only Bruce could see it!' (He used to be the editor of the *Times Literary Supplement*), so I gave her the typed copy I had.

Enid Starkie wrote to me about George. I'd told her how you felt about the nine months in Tobruk – that he wasn't thrown away in routine manoeuvres. She says: 'Meg's courage is astounding. But it is terribly hard to face the fact of inevitable poverty all the rest of life, for all the rest of the way.' I know, I know, but it has just come to me what is true of you – 'as poor, yet making many rich'.

By August the practical side of her nature was uppermost again:

My darlings, my darlings, my days are swifter than a weaver's shuttle, and seem to make the same kind of noise. Somehow the house seems to have had people staying for the night for the last ten days – or else coming for dinner when there wasn't what you would call dinner, so that one was very active in the kitchen. To my amazement I really am becoming a kind of cook – in fact Virginia Gildersleeve* made an 'exclamation upon me',

*Columbia University, New York.

as they say in medieval Latin. I did love having her, for she is a grand, dark-eyed woman, elderly but strong and wise and loves laughing. O.K. completely fell for her. The last visitor was Hilda Morgan, just back from America, a very thin, tired Hilda, but so lovely.

The really exciting thing for me is that I am working on Milton's 'Epitaphium Damonis' for a book that Oxford is doing for Greek famine relief.* And for the first time for months and months and months –

> 'Wakens again the ancient mystery
> The madness and the sacred cry within.'

And I am doing really tolerable work again: and thaw having once set in, I may go on with luck to the book. It is a kind of resurrection, and the odd thing is that it happened all of a sudden on a day of extreme fatigue and depression. I suppose the trough of the wave must be deepest before it begins to rise. Anyhow the strange thing is that doing it, I seem to be doing it for George.

Some weeks intervene and a visit to Kilmacrew, before Helen tells Meg:

I have finished the 'Epitaphium Damonis' all but a little polishing here and there. . . . I think it is good. Anyhow it is the one thing I know of Milton's that has real anguish in it, and I feel quite differently about him. Just as 'Damon' was Milton's camouflage for Charles Deodati, so was this translation for George.

I went yesterday to have tea with Mrs. Shaw and got a dreadful shock, for a tiny figure came out of the drawing-room to meet me, and I could only see the top of its head. She has got that contraction of the spine that sinks your head forward, and it's only when she is sitting that one can see her face. She has grown terribly old, but still a spark of the old intelligence comes out. And I never seen anything so moving as the way old

*Helen probably changed her mind and substituted an article on Cyrenaica.

> G.B.S. – very frail, very thin – waits on her – coaxing her to eat. 'Will you have a piece of bread if I put jam on it?' And he carefully spreads a piece and brings it to her, and she looks up at him – I nearly broke down and cried in the street coming away, that frail pair clinging together in this strange avalanche of a world, and G.B.S., the cynic and the wit, showing only that almost agonised care and tenderness. O.K. always said he was the kindest heart in the world and I could believe it after yesterday. He was talking superbly, in the intervals, and then he would break it off to lift her handkerchief, or guide her cup to the little table. O.K. had asked him to lunch, but he refused. 'I don't like her to have her meals alone . . . she is too much alone, anyhow, with my work keeping me so absorbed. . . .'

Unfortunately work in Constable's offices increased, partly from shortage of staff due to wartime regulations and commandeering, but more from O.K.'s and Voigt's discussions on military strategies, not to mention their reactions to every atom of news on radio or in the press.

When Helen returned from an autumn visit to Kilmacrew she found: 'F.A.V. overjoyed to have me back at office, which was exactly like a wastepaper basket and he rustling in it like an anxious terrier.'

But she could not always see the funny side of him. A particular occasion is recorded when 'F.A.V. had written lightheartedly', –

> 'Gandhi is an evil creature', and had sent off the last pages of MS before I'd seen them, it being very urgent stuff. Proofs came back so late on Monday evening that O.K. says we all three go out to dinner and correct afterwards. I have grave misgivings, but a party is always a party, and it is agreed we come back early. My dear, it was 11 p.m. when we came up these office stairs again. I was almost dead with fatigue, and dinner an interminable political discussion, amicable but a trifle exhausting, above all as I wanted to creep back to the office and get on with the proofs. I spotted the Gandhi thing half-way through and made a mental note to tell F.A.V. it was a match in a tank of

petrol and a crazy thing to do. He was correcting similar proofs next door, but suddenly cab was announced to take us all to London Bridge to get them off by midnight train, and in final scramble I forgot all about Gandhi. Got home about 1 a.m. and crawled to bed: had to alter whole set-up next morning as F.A.V. had run into so many pages. Suddenly late that evening it came from nowhere into my mind – 'Gandhi is an evil creature', and I uttered a short shriek and got wildly busy stopping press at Tonbridge, persuading O.K. of its insanity, strategically anyhow, and getting F.A.V. at dawn next morning to consent to its being deleted. He was completely lamb-like and really grateful, but I was very nearly dead. A thing like that revives so many things in one's head – the incredible tactlessness and blundering when any one government tries to govern an alien people.

P.S. O.K. beginning to talk vaguely about going for a holiday, but I fear it will be like last year, the summer gone before it happens.

Bronze memorial plaques for Jack and George were placed in Magherally Presbyterian Church by the congregation, and portraits of their two sons were given to the parents. Helen writes about the presentation ceremony:

I think it is a marvellous idea to give the balance to the Imperial War Graves Commission: for it is strange to think that they will be doing that ancient divine act of charity (for which Antigone died) to all the men who went to the ends of the earth, and left their mortality there. Charlie says the lettering for the bronzes is beautiful, but nothing should interfere with the austerity of the bronze. If it could be a compromise; if the portraits could be set against the seat back, below the bronzes, so that anyone who liked could see them afterwards, and John Waddell* (or whoever will do the indicating of the bronzes) just mention them. I imagine it will be part of John's sermon.

I have been racking my brains to remember about Jack's

*The Reverend John Waddell, a cousin.

letters. I do remember copying out the marvellous one about flying above the clouds for Dean Kerr, but that came to Elizabeth* after the memorial service.

My darling, November – is November.
''Tis the year's midnight, and it is the day's,'

But it is redeemed not only by –

'He is that fallen lance that lies as hushed . . .
If we who sight it . . .
See nothing worthy to have been its mark,
It is like men who look too near . . .
But this we know, the obstacle that checked
And tripped the body, shot the spirit on
Further than target ever showed or shone.'

*Jack's wife.

CHAPTER XIX

Last Years of War

Although for Helen the years to the end of the war were not to hold any more direct personal bereavements, they were not to be years of refreshment. The lines of endurance and suffering began to appear on her face, and her hair whitened as her physical strength deteriorated. She began to realise that even her imagination could not parry all the 'powers of darkness'. She carried on with an outward show of cheerful courage that deceived even her closest friends into faith that time and the end of the war would bring back her old self, and that she would write and speak again with her old perfection.

An episode in the summer of 1943 when General de Gaulle asked her to translate for him did hearten her effectively for a time, but she made the mistake of refusing payment for her work. She was told that he could never ask her again. She merely shook her head. She could not take money: she was proud to do anything for him. But General de Gaulle too had his brand of pride, and he invited her to lunch at the Savoy Hotel instead.

Helen sent Meg a copy of her translation of the speech General de Gaulle made at Tunis on the morning of Sunday June 27th 1943, and also an account of the luncheon party:

> I send you this translation, because I think the speech is a tremendous bit of work, and the translation not too dusty, (F.A.V. frightfully excited about it. He said a lot to O.K. about how marvellous a thing I had made of it) and also because it explains a delay in writing to my everloving family.
>
> They were so anxious at the French H.Q. that I should do it, and when I read de Gaulle's original I felt the most awful mess

could be made of it. It is so easy to slop over into sentiment, and the feeling here was so passionate. The last sentence took as long as the whole of the rest of it put together.

(The text of the last two paragraphs from Helen's translation follow.)

To France, to Notre Dame la France, this and this only have we to say today: that nothing is of moment to us, nothing of concern to us, except to serve her. Our duty towards her is as simple, as elementary, as the duty of sons towards a mother made captive. We have to set her free, to fight the enemy and chastise the traitors who brought her to this bitter pass, to secure her friends, to snatch the gag from her mouth and the chains from her limbs, so that her voice may again make itself heard, and she go forward on her road to destiny.

Of her we have nothing to ask, save perhaps this: that on the Day of Deliverance she find it in her heart to open to us a mother's arms and let us weep for joy there: and on the day when death will come to take us, she shroud us in her kind and holy earth.

She later describes the Savoy lunch:

Thursday, July 9 1943.

My darling, I have just come back from lunch at the Savoy with the de Gaulle's – the General, and Madame who is enchanting. The General I adore – it is difficult not to, as he is so large and rather like a good sad dog. He was very sweet, and said that his speech was very much finer in my English than his French. About 10 of us at lunch, a couple of ambassadors, and a charming Scot, Lord Sempill (19th Baron, since sometime in the 15th century), who made a sudden speech over coffee and brandy – and presented de Gaulle with a very ancient ring, and spoke of the ancient bonds between Scotland and France. And then to my stark horror de Gaulle looked down the table to where I was sitting and said: 'Et Mademoiselle – de quel pays êtes-vous? Veuillez bien nous parler un peu.' Mercifully extremity brings inspiration. I told them I was 'Irelandaise'; that my country, like France, knew what it was to be enemy to England – 'sweet enemy' – that the wild geese – 'les oies sauvages', had fled after Limerick to the refuge of all free minds, France: and now it was the French who were the wild geese, and had found their refuge in England. For England, horribly inarticulate as she is, has so utterly good a heart: that she has always been in love with France, as a man loves a woman, delighted by her, but bewildered, never understanding what she is after. 'Is not that our power, Madame de Gaulle? (Which brought down the house.) But that it is the woman's business to understand, to make allowances for the large, blundering, inarticulate creature: and so must France with England.

With my wonted modesty, I may say it was a WOW: and how I ever got it all into French I do not know. A lot of Frenchmen came to me on my departing and spoke with great emotion many things I did not follow: and the Sempills came up, and I found she was Sir John Lavery's daughter, and he thinks *The Wandering Scholars* the greatest book ever written and so on and so on – all the result, I think, of the excellent cognac. I am sure that was why I was able to talk French – a little more and I would probably have gone on to Polish.

And I was in such a panic before starting, almost ill at the horrid prospect of stumbling in bad French through a long lunch party. Well, well.

The atmosphere of tense and drawn out suspense put everyone on edge with impatience, especially those whose daily work was based on responsible efforts to interpret the kaleidoscope that was war in 1943 and after.

Helen had nursed Voigt through a bad attack of influenza in the spring of 1944. She had taken him into her own house for a fortnight, and in the first week he had burst three rubber hot-water bottles under the impression that their purpose was to be sat on. (Fortunately he remarried early in 1944).

Helen describes him in July:

Poor F.A.V. is in extremis with a leader on Yugoslavia. Poland, he says, was difficult enough, but the race antagonisms there are a spider's web, and he feels a trapped fly. Poor dear, he had meant to go down to the country for a fortnight to finish his book, but here he still is, with beads of sweat on his head, and tired eyes, with the last page (how well I know it!) still refusing to be reached. Myself at the moment am so stupid that I am not trying. My mind is dank flannel. O.K. went last night after dinner to comfort poor Edward Hutton for the bombardment risk to Rome, and I went out to garden and cut grass with the bread knife till about eleven, when even the young pullets mounted the little stairs to bed.

It is really disconcerting in middle age to realise the enormous flaws in the passionately held conclusions of one's youth. I think it was our dear Jacques who said somewhere that democracy gone wrong had made the bed for dictators. The great thing is to do something: to recite the Lord's Prayer by rote if one's heart is 'withered like the grass' and incapable of devotion. Body and soul are so inextricably interwoven that the discipline of action may have some power on the spirit, the reluctant slug of a spirit. Hence perhaps the sacraments. Hence perhaps the Incarnation.

Charlotte, G. B. Shaw's wife, died in September 1943 and O.K. wanted me to do an obituary notice on her, which I did, but had to leave Bates (O.K.'s secretary) to type, and when I saw it in *The Times* next morning, it was full of misprints – one really dreadful one. You know, she was a very daring rider to hounds in her youth, and I'd written about her courage: 'she shirked none of her fences, from youth to her old age – and faced this last of them with anticipation rather than dread – eager and unwearied in the search for knowledge, wherein her vigorous soul is now satisfied'. Poor Bates wrote 'fancies' for 'fences'. She never shirked her fancies. I was in despair, but O.K. wrote to G.B.S., and he wrote back the kindest note to thank me, and say it didn't really matter, that it made quite good sense, even for the people too stupid to make the correction themselves. Dear G.B.S., he might easily have been so enraged, for she was the least fanciful of women. And to make a fool of her on the day they were burying her (only G.B.S. and the faithful Miss Patch to be at the funeral) was more than I could face.

Even in 1943 some social distractions came Helen's way. A dinner-party is mentioned with Leonard Woolley, the archaeologist, and 'the delightful Brockington', Canadian lawyer and broadcaster, a true friend until her death. There was also a lunch party given by Viola Garvin and the Greek Minister of Information, at which the special guest was 'the great Finn, Tancred Borenius,* whom I adored; he is so like a bulldog and extremely flattering about my immortal works. The last thing I expected from so peremptory and authoritative a man. His real job is art criticism, but like so many people not of our race, he seems to know the literature of every country in Europe and to be intelligent about them.'

A year later, in July 1944, trouble came from a new and unexpected source. In Helen's words:

> . . . A fierce attack was made on the XIXTH by Brendan Bracken – you'll see the bald facts in the new XIXTH when it comes – followed up by one of the most lying attacks I've ever seen in the News Chronicle – quotation chiefly from F.A.V., taken out of context and given the necessary twist and setting. It was so convincing that I sat dizzy and said: 'Can I possibly have let things like that get into the XIXTH and made no protest?' F.A.V. himself blinked a little and looked like something bewildered, confronted with a nightmare of himself! So I got busy on the originals for almost a week, cold black anger mounting in me at the foulness of the thing and its ingenuity.

*Tancred Borenius (1885–1948), Finnish art historian, Professor of the History of Art, University of London from 1922.

And when I'd done my analysis, it went to the firm's lawyer – and he said it was an absolute 'sitter' – malicious libel. So writs are being issued, and I suppose the case will come on in the autumn. But oh my love, anger is very exhausting, and so is exact research and comment combined with it!

The case did not come up till the war was over: O.K. was called as a witness, but Helen was not involved. 'Malicious libel' was given against the accused: it was a triumph for Constable's, a great relief for Helen, and an untold one for F.A.V., whose reputation had already begun to be impaired by his advocacy of General Mihajlovic as against General Tito of Yugoslavia.

Helen dragged her frayed nerves and frail body on and on until in August 1944, after a gruelling spell of close weather and a phoney charwoman, who made off with her purse and O.K.'s gold watch, she finally collapsed in the office.

. . . was taken home by alarmed O.K. in taxi – Voigt anxiously hovering. But Dr. James very reassuring, said heart all right, only dog-tired, take it easy and have a holiday. And kind Monica came and cooked dinner, and I stayed in bed and now am top of the world. And O.K., who has been vainly trying to find any place in England where one can so much as put a toe in, suddenly said: 'Canterbury!' It was because they have set to music one of the greatest things in the *Medieval Latin Lyrics* – 'Phalanx and Squadrons of the Prince-Archangels', and the Dean asked me to come down and hear it at a festival on the 16th of September. That was this morning, and now it is all fixed. . . . Oh my darling, I have always craved that you and I should be in Canterbury together. It is the English Chartres. Could you, could you come?

Two weeks' holiday in Canterbury did restore Helen, and though Meg could not join them she is told:

You have been with me since the first evening we went down a little lane and saw the Cathedral, with such strange effect of radiant stone as it glowed at dusk when everything else is dimmed, from some light inside itself. The stained glass has all been buried for security and the Cathedral is full of light. It might now be the Cathedral of the Holy Ghost: but I remember its rich darkness when I was here for a night ten years ago.

But everything has brought you along with us these days – the nave is like Toulon and Baudet and Avignon and Dijon and Chalons-sur-Saone. And above all Chartres . . . one must never grow too old to go to Chartres. The town is most engaging – not beautiful, but a happy jumble of old overhanging houses and modern plate glass; constant surprises of antiquity, a river and city gate and houses on the river just like Chartres.

My love, that cheque was just because I couldn't buy you things myself or get them over. You see, my books are selling as they never sold before. I think people have gone homesick for the Middle Ages – for any age that was sure of God, and had some absolute standard. Miss Johnson at the office, who has charge of the paper, says they could sell thousands more if only they had paper.

After her return to Primrose Hill Helen writes quietly: 'I am still very husky and bobbish', and continues with items of her social news:

Did I tell you that Rachel Voigt, F.A.V.'s new wife, had to be operated on just two weeks after they were married? It was successful and she is about again. They are so happy, and he is so gentle and at peace. A nice Polish friend came in two days ago and said: 'What has happened to Mr. Voigt? He looks like a little boy who was lost, and has come home?'

And in another letter:

Mollie says you never got a letter of mine about Alec Glendinning being alive, and in a camp in Malaya. The Jap general in charge of Singapore is a Christian and an Oxford man, and reported very humane, so Alec may be tolerably fixed. News came through someone writing to the Red Cross in Switzerland. Hedli, his sister, is married to Louis MacNeice and expecting a baby in the early summer. . . . Did I tell you that Michael Sadleir has lost his elder son, Tom? He was in the Motor Gun Boats, and killed in a scrap at sea. Poor Michael, he looks suddenly like an old man.

I don't know why it seems almost impossible to write. I sometimes think the din of outside things is so tremendous, and to communicate at all is like shouting meaningless things in a noisy tram, or a crowded railway carriage. Yet letters from you and Mollie are such an ecstasy to get, and mine are so poor in return.

I have been seeing a good deal of O.K.'s niece, Katherine, who married Sydney Chapman, an astronomer. Their son Robert arrives to take me out to lunch sometimes, because he enormously admires my books. . . . It was to please him I went to lecture at his old school. Unfortunately it was my first night fire-watching down here, so I didn't feel my brightest going down to Wimbledon; but they were very civil about the lecture. Never again, said I, and have just refused to lecture in Cambridge on 'Paris University in the Middle Ages' in February. It tempted me, but I just can't do it. Life crowds up so on me, even trifles.

The winter months of 1944 were days of great danger from the sky. Hitler's last hope lay in destroying London and the Channel ports by high-powered rockets (V2s). The damage they caused was devastating indeed, as they could neither be seen nor heard until they crashed with a last-second scream. And the occasional flying-bomb still reached England from launching-pads in Holland and Belgium.

On 25th November 1944 a lonely V1 fell in King Henry's Road, Hampstead. A day or two earlier, in nearby Primrose Hill Road, a crack had appeared on a wall in O.K.'s room: Helen insisted on his sleeping in the old basement kitchen, and she quotes him as saying: 'I always said I wanted to sleep in the kitchen and at last I am allowed to.' She herself was sleeping in the little 'oakroom', which she claimed the late Mr Buzzard (of wedding-cake fame) had made his den because of its Adam ceiling and oak beams. She wrote a particularly long letter to Meg about the night of that close V1:

> My dear, it was so strange a thing. You know that like you I am a middling sleeper and given to what they call 'night exercises' in the army. I'd wakened, and finally gone down to prowl and rake the damn boiler, which is a good dear boiler, not its fault, but the coke. Came back to bed, accompanied by Toty, who seemed to wish for company, put out the light and meditated. Then heard a swish, and like any b.f. instead of hauling pillow over my head, sat up thinking 'Now I'll see the flash'. I am almost ashamed to relate it, it is so far from what one is told to do, and so unlike what I have often done before – for I always have an enormous cushion by my bed in case of flying glass. Then came the indescribable, a sense of rushing, tearing fury, a noise that must have been composed of the crash of houses some gardens away, the descent of a lot of my own ceiling, and the crash of a wardrobe on the floor above, and of most of the glass and ceilings in the house, all in a strange swoop of sound and rage and shrillness. The incredible thing is that I have often been afraid before, but now not at all; I can only remember a kind of horror at this bestial violence – the rebellion of the sane mind against the beast. It was like a tiger tearing, clawing at the house. And then I said to myself 'Now the walls will come in', and sat there waiting. And they didn't. And then I put on the lamp, and groped under the bed for my bedroom slippers and cursed domestic help who always tucks them into show cupboard miles away across the room – now a sea of mortar and splintered glass. I could hear O.K. moving, shouting 'Are you all right?' and going up to Elizabeth Lucas, who was in Rosamond's room (one window and crashed sideboard and hole in partition wall the only trouble there), and on up to Miss Matthews, who met him quite composed and very elongated in a long white nightgown. Meantime I'd followed

the ancient custom of making paths for my feet by hurling eiderdown, blanket, cushion, as a kind of causeway to the door, and O.K. coming down again saying: 'Are you all right?' Heard a necessary: 'All right, but for pity's sake bring me some slippers!' Then we all assembled in the old kitchen, and had tea and brandy and the others went back to bed, but I, as if I were an old hand, decided the one important thing was to clear the glass and rubble out of the kitchen sink, or we'd have a stopped sink for our comfort, and did so. Then I came back to my room and turned on the light, and saw on my pillow the corner of the Adam ceiling resting on its point. It had come down behind me when I sat up, and in the general roar and rush I had noticed nothing. If I hadn't been a fool and sat up, it would have finished me, for when I tried to lift it off my pillow I couldn't. If I hadn't been awake . . . neither O.K. nor Elizabeth Lucas wakened till the crash came, nor the ladies upstairs. So, my heart, I have an odd feeling that Providence intends me to use my useless head a little longer. I am telling you this, because I think now you won't be frightened any more.

Hitler's 'secret weapons' continued spasmodically until the launching-pads had been destroyed by the R.A.F., or by the advances of the Allied Armies. Yet as late as March 21st 1945, Helen's front windows were blown out again by a rocket that landed near the guns on Primrose Hill, and once more all was 'fatigue, confusion and rubble', for the War Damage Committee had not finished repairing the far more serious destruction of the previous November. A friend who visited Helen commented at the time: 'I am heart-sad about her. Her domestic troubles with the bomb damage are altogether too much for her. It is tragic to see.'

There is a gap in Helen's letters to her sister and then they begin again:

Darling, forgive these last silent weeks, I just was dead. There were nights I crawled to bed so tired I couldn't undress and just dropped asleep where I lay.

O.K.'s room, the one civilised room in the house through it all, (except the old kitchen), has suddenly decided to have an unsafe wall after all, and last Monday I carried books out for most of the day. I was determined his shouldn't suffer the ruin of mine. O.K. has been so patient with all the dirt and confusion, bless him, but so downhearted that he has no strength to move things or do things for himself; even the coke buckets are too much for him. But he keeps fairly well. . . .

Darling I had sunk into such apathy, that was why I wrote so little. Why send you letters like withered grass? I used to write and tear them up. Besides censorships send them back if one mentions anything about damage, and that discouraged me.

We go back to town today after four blessed days. And soon, soon, surely, surely, I'll see you and the turn of the road to Kilmacrew again.

At last V.E. day dawned. Helen actually dated her letter – 6th May, 1945.

Darling, my darling,

It's between 4 p.m. and 5 p.m. and the tension in the street grows every minute. I'm in the office and Constable's have found their Union Jack and just managed to get it out of a window on a flat post. I ransacked a cupboard before I left home and found the flags, and yards of bunting which I hurriedly washed and left my woman to iron, and I'll hang it up when I go home. The strange thing is that though there is relief everywhere, there isn't much gaiety. There has been too much killing, too much death. And I find myself remembering –

'O hands that made them,
Gather the ashes in.'

I couldn't think why I was so haunted by you when I was looking for the flags and the bunting, almost turning to speak to you over my shoulder, and I have just remembered we got them for George V, and his Jubilee in 1935, and you were here, and we drove everywhere and it was such fun – ten years, ten years.

And my darling, this day of all days, I must write to you.

The case has been postponed to June 4th. When it's over, I believe, I really believe, that O.K. will come away. Let's think of the first week of July, and the benediction of the long twilights, and you, my love, and you.

I am suddenly well again, because the doctor got me something that made me sleep like a log and yet waken as clear as a clean window.

CHAPTER XX

Fragments that Remain

The collapse of the enemy in Europe, the fall of Berlin, the suicide of Hitler and his minions were finalised in April 1945. In England relief was paramount, not elation, not triumph. May 6th was quite unlike November 11th 1918, perhaps because World War II had revealed that more unspeakable depths of brutality and degradation could be reached and tolerated by mankind under the guise of wartime necessity.

Peace did mean the removal of fear of telegrams from the War Office and of bombs from the sky. Lights did go up in streets and windows, bringing friendly smiles to eyes and hearts after years of gloomy, oppressive darkness. Slowly but gradually relief became positive determination to restore, renovate and improve; but many were the individuals so prematurely aged by suffering that their vitality had been sapped beyond recovery.

Helen seemed among those for whom hope was justified. Plans to set her free from *The Nineteenth Century* depended on the demobilisation of survivors of Constable's staff. Alec Glendinning was expected to resume his old post as assistant to Voigt. He was known to have escaped from Singapore, but as time passed and nothing more was ever heard of him, his death had to be presumed. Helen mentions the return of Ralph Arnold 'back from Ceylon, very thin and quiet but awfully anxious to be in Orange Street again. He comes on Monday, and being in taste and gentleness more in O.K.'s tradition than any of them, I feel he will act as a kind of bodyguard and understudy combined.'

It took six months to find a successor to Helen, and, after her release from office drudgery, she did turn back to her own creative work. She collected the poems she had translated during the war, and it is impossible not to feel that if she had been adequately supported, she would have corrected and polished them into the book she had planned. The Introduction and a list of contents remain among her papers, and the text of the poems is in her notebooks.

Her MSS of *John of Salisbury* might have been saved too. Her intense interest in him was based on his connection with Abelard. John had been one of the renowned teacher's star students, and had attended his last lectures before his retirement to Cluny. Her paper on John for the English Association had been published by the Clarendon Press of Oxford in 1928, and by 1938 she told Meg she had finished a rough draft of a full-length book and that she had been 'cheered also by the publication of a book on Bartholomew of Exeter, friend of John of Salisbury, which is not only full of exact and unimportant (but to me absorbing) information, but so incredibly dull that I find I am quite a good writer.

John of Salisbury and Latin dictionary came in O.K.'s taxi this morning and sit very academic and important on shelf.'

But a few weeks later her tone is less optimistic. Writing from Ventnor, where she and O.K. were having a brief holiday, to Meg who had been unable to join them:

> Darling, this place is always haunted by you, and indeed I wish you had packed up and come. Somehow it seems to cure me of all my ills. It's the high downs and the sea I think. I am not speaking the broadcast on the 27th for my voice is very uncertain yet – all the carrying notes gone – and anyhow they so sickened me wanting extra voices to make this passage dramatic, and to sing this piece and read that. I finally told them they could have the material and work it up as they pleased, for I hadn't any more time to spend on it. I am sorry I ever said I would do it, for it made the last few weeks such a strain, and ruined any chance of finishing John of Salisbury. But it's all peaceful in my mind now.

Before quoting from Helen's Introduction to her unpublished wartime poems, where she tells how she renounced the idea of the book on *John of Salisbury*, I have included below some poignant recollections of this time. They are taken from a letter to Enid Starkie written by Madame de Praingy, daughter of the famous Dr Vaudremer, who was so particularly kind to Helen when she was ill in Paris in 1924. Enid Starkie, Nicole de Praingy and Helen remained friends for over forty years.

My dear Enid, Paris. 9th October 1967

The other evening you asked if I had material or letters of Helen's. Unfortunately the war and its misfortunes destroyed all the things I treasured most. . . . You asked me to try and recall my memories of Helen. . . . I was near her in London at the time of the re-occupation of the Ruhr by the Germans. . . . Helen had written *The Desert Fathers* whom she loved dearly, and I seem to recollect that it was then she began to talk about John of Salisbury. . . . But then the war broke out and four terrible years ensued for everyone, and there was complete silence between both families. How greatly I rejoiced in 1945 at the chance of a journey to London to see you all! . . . Helen and Mr. Kyllmann met me at Victoria Station. She had a chronic cold in her head, but she, weeping in deep depression, confided to me that her one wish was to complete her work on John of Salisbury, only the small jobs and calls on her paralysed her for any concentrated big work of her own. . . . The tragic moment for her was when she realised that her mental faculties had begun to fail, and that she would never achieve this book on John of Salisbury which lay so close to her heart. I saw her again in 1952; and I see her now as she sat with her hands folded on her knees in her sitting-room in front of a small picture of Christ stumbling under the burden of His Cross. With tears in her eyes she said: 'My cross is very heavy too and is crushing me, but, looking at Him, I try to carry it without being too complaining and sorry for myself.' . . . I think that if Helen's notes that she gleaned on John of Salisbury could be retrieved, it would be great if they are coherent enough for a small book.

And the *Translator's Note* which Helen wrote as a Preface to her unpublished book of poems:

In the early days of September 1938, I was working on John of Salisbury, Thomas Becket's secretary; the academic Ciceronian scholar forced by his conscience into the age-long struggle between Church and State, and disapproving the intransigence of both. His letters made good reading for an outmoded Liberal. 'Consider,' he wrote, 'that point of time when Caligula – I know not whether sloughing or perfecting the dictator, having done all things, engulfed all things. The image of that time often occurs to me, when all the affairs of the subjects are disposed at one strong man's nod; and these subjects prepared, albeit with shrinking soul, to pronounce sentence of exile, or death, against themselves. *Hinc inde potestas terribilis*; hence a terrible power. To this pitch indeed, that the priests dissemble the precepts of the divine law, that men are old without wisdom, that a judge sits ignorant of law, a prelate knows nothing of authority or his people of discipline, that a man free born shall spurn his liberty, and a whole nation its quiet and its peace.'

I had not long finished translating this paragraph from the 'Polycraticus' when the Governments of England and France prevailed on Czechoslovakia to surrender her western frontier to the Third Reich.

The months that followed were not happy, even for those more rich in hope; it was difficult for anyone to support the spectacle of the guaranteed frontiers slipping, like the battlements one makes with spade and bucket, into the incoming tide. It was an ugly winter in London, full of illness and ill news. But midway in January came the first pale spring Sunday of the year; some of us, thirsty for music drifted into an afternoon concert. I have forgotten the player's name, and I sat where I saw nothing but the reflection of his hands in the dark mirror of the Bechstein at which he played. I had been brooding, not happily, on the power of physical violence to cripple men's minds, and on this new evil doctrine of enslaving the arts to the State: and suddenly the free movement of those hands against darkness became a symbol.

> 'Even as a bird
> Out of the fowler's snare
> Escapes away.
> So is our soul set free.
> Rent is their net,
> And thus escaped we.
>
> I saw the shadow of the player's hands
> Against all Europe.
> Against all time
> I saw the shadow of the player's hands.'

In that moment of liberation a forgotten memory of Alcuin came to me, the fragment on the Lombard occupation of Rome that begins:

> 'By these, by these same chains, O Rome. . . .'

and ends

> 'That road is closed to war, whose gate
> Stands open to the stars.'

I knew then that I must for the time abandon John of Salisbury and translate these things that I had read once and commended and forgotten 'in those first years when youth in me was happy and life was swift in doing, and I wandering in the divers cities of sweet France'; when the peace was not half a decade old and Locarno shone over Europe like a harvest moon, not yet a paper lantern with its sides stove in, and the laments for Aquileia and for Lindisfarne and Boethius' counsel to his own soul seemed brave things indeed, but remote as the inscriptions in ancient graveyards.

For the poems themselves I make no great claim, even in the original Latin, still less in translation. Their value lies not in the quality of their poetry, but in their courage and their poignancy; indeed in their bare existence. They are like the inscriptions scratched on dungeon walls or prison windows, the defiance of the spirit of man against material circumstance. Alcuin's lament for the sack of Lindisfarne by the Northmen seemed to me when I read it years ago a little trite, and full of ancient platitude; now that the bombers circle over Holy Island, I read it with a kind of contemporary anguish. 'By these, by these same chains' was strong consolation, when the banners of the swastika moved through the streets of Prague.

Boethius' *Consolation of Philosophy*, indeed, is in a different category: in every century men have listened to it, heard in it a kind of Angelus rung in the evening of the ancient world. Yet one read it with a detached romantic sensibility, even as at sixteen one construed the autumnal prose of Cicero and Laetius conversing of friendship and old age and death; read it as Boethius himself admits he used to read philosophy in his library, with its walls of ebony and ivory. But when the veiled figure stands beside him in the dungeon at Pavia, looking upon him with more than mortal eyes, the moment of recognition is not for him only. Pavia becomes Dachau; the senator's toga a German pastor's dress. 'Whoever he be,' wrote John of Salisbury, 'that is willing to suffer for his faith, whether he be little lad or man grown, Jew or Gentile, Christian or Infidel, man or woman, it matters not at all: who dies for justice dies a martyr, a defender of the cause of Christ.'

Medieval Latin poetry, read in these days, has something of the quality of the eleventh chapter of the Epistle to the Hebrews: '*These all died in faith, not having received the promises . . . that they without us should not be made perfect.*' If there is melancholy in the realisation that the wisdom and kindness of mankind has profited the world so little, it is that we are still in Newton's square box of a universe: that Boethius' definition of eternity, 'the possession of all time, past, present, and to come, in full plenitude, in one single moment, here and now' is seldom hazarded in our experience. Yet by these things men live, and in them is the life of our spirit.

CHAPTER XXI

The W. P. Ker Eighth Memorial Lecture

Shortly after the war ended Glasgow University invited Helen to give their most important lecture: she accepted with delight and chose the subject of 'Latin Poetry in the Dark Ages'.* The original date fixed was for the autumn of 1946, but influenza intervened, and it was October 1947 before her vulnerable throat recovered enough to assure her the use of her voice to full effect. (Helen knew she could hold an audience spellbound and enraptured by the music of her voice alone.)

The winter of 1946–7, when fuel was scarce and frost and snow severe, produced weeks of hardship from cold. Pipes froze not only inside and outside houses and buildings, but also under the streets, thus blocking the flow from mains. Hampstead High Street had to be dug up and the Primrose Hill district was not spared. Helen's reaction brought an apology to Meg:

> Darlings, I have so neglected you, but the cold and the cuts have made all the small taken-for-granted business of life so complicated that night is on me before I know. Also I have been working on my lecture in dots and dashes and am now not frightened. For so long I have been in despair that my mind couldn't get to the heat where it sparks. I could accumulate facts in rows, like the little balls on an adding machine, and they would have added up to a lecture. But the wind never blew. And now at last, when the savage cold had made me utterly despair, it suddenly blew yesterday, and I worked like somebody cutting corn on a hot day.

*See page 222 for complete text.

By the spring of 1947 Helen and O.K. were desperately needing a holiday, and Meg is asked:

> Could you have us for a while? O.K. is terribly tired and longing for Kilmacrew. . . . I am cheerfuller every day, and above all now that I know it will do Glasgow just as well if I lecture in the autumn. It's a good lecture and I see a book coming out of it. I want to do a really great translation of the Second Book of the Aeneid – Aeneas telling the story of the night Troy fell – it is just London burning.
>
> And slowly, slowly I'm finding all the books I want. Monica begs me to use the British Museum as little as I can for a few months. She says it is like going into an old Italian or French church. (Do you remember that one at Vézélay?) It will dry out in time, but she got a vicious cold in August. I'll wait till I have a list of queries and then make a day of it in a fur coat!
>
> Mrs. Ferris* wants me to give away the prizes at Victoria School the week after the Queen's College do, but I'm begging off. I'll do it some other time, but I do so loathe public appearances. The one thing about lunch is that I shall have to buy a new hat, and what a purgatory that is. Mercifully for Glasgow the lecture, though an afternoon one, means a gown, and if I must appear in a mortarboard it can be removed at once. I am so happy about that lecture: the whole thing is growing like a tree. It begins with the ill-fated arrogance of Claudius.

Early in the autumn Helen begged for Mollie to come over and help her look after O.K. and 'all the small things that cluster up my head'. Mollie went to her rescue and obviously saved the situation in Primrose Hill. But there were other pressures besides O.K., and Helen finishes a letter with:

> And finally I have had such a mass of exacting letters, including one from the Ministry of Information to supply the medieval section of a film they are doing on England. (Answer in the negative). And I think all the societies in Oxford and

*The headmistress of Victoria School for Girls, Belfast.

Cambridge asked me to lecture on this or that in the autumn term, all in such warm language that an individual civil and warming reply was essential. Yesterday I suddenly knew that I would write again, and really write, not just enough to 'pass myself' in a lecture where your voice can get away with so much. It was heaven for a moment. And then I went down to a dreadful scullery, full of all kinds of leftovers and what not, and I still remembered.

I am to lecture in Glasgow on October 28th, but no longer dread it, and am staying with Barbara Vere-Hodge in Edinburgh.

Helen gratefully acknowledged her debt to Mollie after her journey to Glasgow had proved a flawless success, which had to be shared with Meg as soon as possible:

My darling, you have been so neglected, but I was in a kind of aquarium the last few weeks, and so grateful for Mollie. I just don't know how I'd have done the last fusing of material: it isn't that there is so much to do in the house, it's only the constant interruption. You can't get *Sunk*. I worked most of the way up to Edinburgh on an MS that had been so written and rewritten, bitted and pieced, till it looked like a roll of crumpled paper.

I finally followed Sir Hector Hetherington* and the Mace Bearer to the platform feeling like Charles I stepping out of the window at Whitehall. But after that it was easy – it's like the panic of stepping off into deep water. We'd had lunch with the Hetheringtons (he is a delightful creature, white-haired and massive but still mischievous), and she is very sweet. Then we had to go to tea at the University Club, and I talked wildly to everybody – and then back to the Hetheringtons for a brief interval. Then down to the Central Station Hotel to have an early dinner with Eric Linklater, and then to the reception at 7.30, when to my horror I had to speak again; and then a train back to Edinburgh. We got back to Barbara's lovely 18th cen-

*Principal of Glasgow University.

tury house about half past eleven, I talking all the way from Glasgow to an old friend from Oxford now teaching in Edinburgh.

But dear Buni (nickname for the Professor of Tropical Diseases who is Barbara's husband) was waiting up, a kettle boiling for tea, which he laced with rum. He is a most lovable creature, sandy, sardonic and so incredibly kind and wise. I stayed next day, and Barbara drove me round Edinburgh, with which I am in love as with a foreign city.

The things they said about me in Glasgow – Sir Hector at the lecture and Eric Linklater at the P.E.N. Club reception were so fantastically untrue that I don't remember them, but you, my darling, would have lapped them up and been so happy to hear your sister described in such proud language. I travelled most of Thursday and got back so thankfully to my ever-loving family and a blazing fire. Alas, by Sunday morning my old faithful laryngitis ('the laryngitis of exhaustion' as Papa Vaudremer used to say) had damped down on me and I thankfully stayed in bed and am still there, but hope to bounce up tomorrow. It is heaven to be in bed, and to know somebody is getting dinner for O.K. and breakfast too. I was almost speechless yesterday, but the soreness is very much gone today, and temperature almost normal. But that finishes me for lectures.

Mrs Vere Hodge wrote a letter to O.K. describing the event, which pleased them both enormously:

28 Ann Street
Edinburgh
4 Nov. 1947

My dear O.K.,

I meant to write to you last week: the days have somehow melted and my letter has just stayed in my head. But though it comes late to you, I think you will like to have an account of this hour last week, from someone who was made glad by Helen's triumph, and who wished all the time that you were sitting beside her to share it!

For it was a triumph, O.K., and I think that everyone who sat in that crowded lecture hall will remember the wisdom and beauty of what she said. It made me glad to see how many of the young ones were there, and to feel them warm to her voice, and respond to the wisdom and the renewed hope she gave them. One had the conviction that something undying and eternal was being transmitted to another generation – the essence of that spirit that went with the 'young things gathered up for exile' was being conserved and passed on through the centuries.

Helen came in with such grace and dignity – with W. P. Ker's robes flowing round her and her white hair shining – I am sure he was proud and delighted by the sight of her. For me it seemed an hour outside time, as if the back and spaces of the hall were filled with shadowy presences – old scholars mingling with the young and living, and all of them sharing the truth and the beauty which Helen presented to them.

It was a great moment in which to share and I felt honoured.

We had a happy and peaceful day on Wednesday, and I hope Helen was not too tired when she got home. We were very loath to let her go, but I hope you may both come back sometime next spring.

Thank you so much for the chocolates, dear O.K. and I send my love.

BARBARA

Helen as usual passed on her reactions to Meg:

. . . I am so comforted. Barbara Vere Hodge wrote to O.K. and he brought the letter to me this evening and Mollie said she would copy it for you, but I wanted to, vain pig that I am, myself. And anyhow I have nothing else to do but cough. I can't do another day's speaking. Voice is just finished and energy too. Mollie is being so dear, so dear. And I'll be all right again soon, throat much better only I do cough so at night. I think I got up too soon, and stayed up too long on Wednesday. . . .

There is a kind of peace on me now. I know what I must *not* do. No more public speaking for me – no more working to a date. Just being a silent mouse, eating its way through paper. It's a pity, having a good voice for broadcasting and all that, but I think it is the lion's roar and the mouse's heart – wasn't there an Aesop fable to that effect?

But Barbara's letter has left me at peace. For though I knew it was all right, I was so weary that I drew my mind away from it as you do from the fatigues of a night's crossing.

After the publication of the W. P. Ker lecture by Glasgow University in 1948, more letters of appreciation poured in to Helen, among them one from Thomas Jones, whose friendship dated from pre-war days and breakfast with Stanley Baldwin. He congratulates her, saying:

> It was such a pleasure to receive at Christmas the Ker lecture: it came just in time to enable me to please numerous friends with copies of it. I pass their thanks on to you – Violet Markham, Mary Glasgow, Lord Macmillan, Ifor Evans, and Co. Mary Glasgow remembered an Oxford lecture on *The Wandering Scholars* – 'in ten minutes we were under a spell whose effects have lasted for me twenty years'.

CHAPTER XXII

Last Efforts

In 1946, following upon her retirement from working at Constable's offices, Helen's letters to her sister became frequent again, and correspondence with her friends was revived. One of these is a note from Stanley Baldwin shortly after the death of his wife:

My very dear Helen,

I cannot reply adequately to your beautiful letter. The Lament from the IXth century ('Thou has come safe to port') is the gem and is of great comfort. I am still stunned and am automatically answering some five hundred letters. But my friends are wonderfully kind and I cling to them.

Yours ever,

S.B.

There are good signs of her recovery in letters from friends, and perhaps most of all from Siegfried Sassoon, with whom a warm friendship had developed after the publication by Constable's of his biography of George Meredith. An earlier letter, written before the end of the war, reveals their mutual interest in each other's work. Helen had sent him a copy of her *Lament for Damian* and he responded:

My Latin is very poor, so Milton's *Epitaphium Damonis* was only known to me by sight in my Baskerville and Pickering editions. Your version is extremely beautiful. And how near it brings him, with his elm and crackling chestnuts. I am most grateful, and am looking forward to showing it to Edmund Blunden next time he comes here.

I am doing my best to repay you with some of my own works. The American edition of *Rhymed Ruminations* is pretty, isn't it? The scrap of prose is from my *Weald of Youth*. Geoffrey Keynes had some 18th century paper, and used it for this little production. Hoping that you will find your way to Wiltshire, and this library, where I am listening to the evening blackbirds.

Two letters from Helen to him, though of a later date, are relevant on the same subject:

Dear Siegfried,

. . . Did you see that one line of your *Mercy* got into the *Times Lit. Sup.* leader, which was also on my W. P. Ker lecture? I missed it in the *Observer*, but whoever did that leader had pounced on it. His theme was the new darkness, quoting Hardy 'In the scene threatened with a new Dark Age', and he goes on . . . 'and when a fine poet of our day suggests to statesmen "methods by mercy bless'd" the ancient word seems to shadow forth an innovation'.

Bless you always. This is the answer to your reluctance to publish.

HELEN

But by November 1946 she is admitting the fluctuations in her health:

My dear Siegfried,

I have been like something lost in a fog for most of the year, and my memory is still full of holes. But I am going to Ireland very soon, to the house that is Denise's house in *Abelard*, and to the sister who is Denise. And when I come back in January I'll be the creature you know. Your *Common Chords* lies on my desk, and today I opened it, strangely at '*The Message*'. I bless you for it.

There isn't anything wrong except anaemia, aggravated by absence of domestic help. . . .

At this point my black cat sat down on my blotter, and he's had to be heavily bribed to remove himself. And in clearing the débris as he went the photograph George took of you, with the glory of fire behind you, came to the surface. How good it is – rather like the Meditations of Marcus Aurelius.

My love always,

HELEN

6th November 1947

My dear Siegfried,

I am peacefully anchored with laryngitis and grateful to it, for I did manage to get to the W. P. Ker lecture given last week, and now I can't talk, and my niece Mollie is here to run the house, and I am in peace. 'The body is very wise.'

O.K. will let me see the proofs of your Meredith; you have made him happy. The first batch of typescript that I read last May was to me so exciting that it was taken from me. But I have always wanted to talk to you about the problem of his (apparent) flippancy and callousness about the publishing of *Modern Love*. I think myself the reason was this; he *must* publish it. You can't refuse, if you are a human being and a writer, to publish the most truthful things, and the one thing of genius, that you have yet done. Or you'd be the man burying 'that one talent which t'were death to hide'. But the passionately *private* side of Meredith must somehow protect itself – like the little creatures who try to hide the nest in the heather by fluttering and crying somewhere else. And the only way to do it is the ironic detachment with which he writes about it – his sardonic indifference accepted for its quality of poetry, and a good 'middle' among work of less weight.

This, at least, is a possible view, and it fits in with the anemone-shrinking sensitiveness that made him understand some of the fortunes of the *Egoist*.

It will be so good to see you, and please God once this bout is over I'll be less Toad-in-the-hole.

My love and blessing

HELEN

Helen's letters to Meg record her fluctuations in body and spirit. She often quoted Thackeray – 'Politics are a thing half real which require an effort of the mind to make them real.' She rebelled against the diet prescribed by O.K. and Voigt at breakfast, at work in the office and at evening meals whether at home or in a restaurant. She had no longer the energy to be a victim.

All her literary life she had been upset when anyone quoted from her published writings without her permission. Gustav Holst gave her a standard for the setting of her lyrics to music: it had to be high to compete with the music of her words. But after *Peter Abelard* became famous the danger of plagiarism was obvious: and the members of Constable's staff kept a keen look-out. Very soon after the war ended a young man pestered her for months. He had been brash enough to adapt *Peter Abelard* for the stage, and to offer it to Alec Guinness without approaching Helen in any way. As she had every intention of adapting her novel herself, and long ago had promised the part of Abelard to Robert Donat, she refused. Her gentle nature faltered at the persistence of the obstinate playwright, but O.K. kept her adamant in refusal.

There were also gayer and more hopeful days to share with Meg. Early in 1947 she starts a letter with:

> O my lambs, I have so much to tell you. Not about myself, being still nose to proofs. The only agreeable thing which will delight you is that I have just been asked if I will judge the Latin verse-speaking in Oxford along with Gilbert Murray who is doing the Greek. And they don't know I daren't quote a line of Virgil without blenching lest I get the quantities all wrong. But how dear of them! I will reply truthfully and quietly.
>
> I have been reading a marvellous book by Dreiser, his last. And here are some quotations from it. The hero is someone rather like our father. . . . 'Men must be honest with God and with themselves. . . . You see, God talks directly to man when His help is needed and man asks him for it. . . . Good intent is of itself a universal language. . . . For the first time in her life subjected to the *weight of spiritual* beauty that is in the lives of

John Woolman* and her father. . . . If thee does not turn to the Inner Light, where will thee go?' Dreiser died a few days after he had finished it.

My darlings, you have been so neglected, but things have piled like a load of hay. A sudden rush job, very exciting but very wearing – the offer to O.K. (as Constable's) of the twenty years or so correspondence between Bernard Shaw and Mrs. Patrick Campbell – the famous actress (as it might be Antony and Cleopatra). Brilliant letters of so strange integrity, for you are convinced that they were deep in love but ran straight. But the agent had to have it back on Monday, and I only got it Friday night. Nearly read myself silly, for it was so exciting and the writing so brilliant, and there was only me to do it, for both Michael and Ralph Arnold were on holiday, and O.K.'s eyes were leaving him pretty helpless: anyhow I got it done and wrote a report – and then sat down and blew like a whale.

Even the diversion of a spectacular marriage hardly raised her flagging spirits:

The only outstanding social event was the wedding of Shirley Morgan to the Marquis of Anglesey – charming dark young man, very sensitive, and very ancient lineage. A wasted day, except that O.K. and I are both so fond of Charles and Hilda.

But oh the crowds, and the mounted police, and dear old Queen Mary looking so benevolent. And a marquee in the grounds of Walpole House (lent by aunt of bridegroom for the occasion) with a seething mob that reminded me more of Dundalk flower-show than of a private entertainment. O.K. and I fled at the earliest possible moment by taking advantage of temporary absence of bride and groom to be photographed with Queen Mary. . . . We came rapturously home agreeing we had seen a lot of old friends, but would rather have seen them somewhere else. And O.K. declared we'd dine at the 'Ivy' and finish the day.

*John Woolman (1720–1772), American Quaker and abolitionist, itinerant preacher inveighing against slavery.

Otto Kyllmann tried in every possible way he could devise (short of leaving London), to encourage Helen to write. Undoubtedly the shortage of paper and the difficulties of publishing had still to be taken into account, but O.K., old and tired as he was, remained an unpractical optimist. He hoped that to see any writing of her own in print would stimulate her to create again, so he suggested the reprinting in book form of the Bible Stories she had contributed to a Belfast religious magazine during the 1914–1918 war. Helen agreed, but her heart was not in them. She longed to see *John of Salisbury* as well as her recent poems and translations in print: they might have infused her with enough energy to write the second volume of *Peter Abelard*, which was always in her mind and heart; and, perhaps, a life of Boethius or Alcuin.

> No appetite and no energy, so just struggled on with replies to essential things, like refusing to lecture to the gentlemen of Westminster School. I'd rather have liked to re-hash the W. P. Ker for them, but once break the tradition I *don't* lecture, and I'm sunk. (Letters still coming in about that lecture, most comforting.) I am sending the 'Daybreak' magazine stories in relays to be typed, and trying *not* to alter, for I've spent hours over one paragraph and resorted to the original in the end.

But when spring came her spirits rose. She was absorbed and declared: 'All day I've been plugging at the old reader, and I think it will be a little jewel. The stories are so lovely now I have cut down all the extras.'

When they were finished Michael Sadleir wrote to her:

> I have read your enchanting stories with rapt enjoyment. They have the lovely simplicity which only the finest workmanship can achieve. . . . The little book is a safe winner. One final point, at the risk of getting a big raspberry, are you convinced that 'Holy Writ' is the right phrase? I cannot help feeling that it is a shade pedantic for such pellucid writing which is like something conjured up from the youth of the world.

And Helen adds: 'I knew Ralph Arnold would like them, and O.K., but that strange, incalculable Michael, so bitter and at times so sweet – and as a rule so impatient of religion. He told O.K. that he adored the early ones, but that St Paul just crashed him. "Michael talks about them as if they had changed his whole life."'

After the publication of *Stories from Holy Writ* Helen tells Meg:

> I think the little book may do all right, but everything seemed to go wrong. It was to have been out early in November. Now it is December, too late for all the Christmas lists and so on, so I don't think it will get any reviewing till after the New Year. People are away at the office and O.K. harried and worried: indeed he forgot to tell me that the North of Ireland B.B.C. are going to do a broadcast on it. However, I've had some marvellous letters about it. There's one letter from Violet Markham – the one that does so much social work – that is worth all the secret disappointments and the small fretting. She begins: 'Only last week I was thinking of you, for I had in my hands the *Desert Fathers* and was remembering the night I read it after laying my husband to rest, and how it gave me the courage to go on. I can't tell you how moved I am by the *Stories from Holy Writ*. I don't think there is any living writer who has your power to say the deepest things in the simplest words'.

The sales of the book, in spite of being brought out too late for Christmas, were enough to make O.K. ring up Helen to say that: 'with practically no reviewing, sales at the moment are something like 3,500 copies, and Macmillans of America are doing the little book there and Longman's are doing it in Canada.'

But success with a youthful reprint could not console Helen for failure to put into words the inspiration of her heart and mind, and she was still clearsighted enough to see but not accept, practical solutions. In a few sad sentences she confides in Meg:

> Darling, I have turned down Chicago and the Aeneid. I thought and thought. Yet I still hesitated, and then I just faced the facts

> – that this hunted existence gives me little time as it is, for work that I always wanted to do: and that the Aeneid would become like a millstone – neither get itself finished nor let me finish anything else. So I sent the letter off by airmail, and then sat down with my head in my hands. Not to weep. It was the first time I had refused a grand piece of work because I knew I had not enough energy left. Did I tell you that Barnard College offered me the first Virginia Gildersleeve Fellowship $4,600 for the half year, lecturing at Barnard? A lovely letter just in from Virginia herself, who had had no hope that I'd take it, but would have liked me to be the first.

A few months later a holiday at Broadstairs braced her up again for less strenuous efforts:

> It suddenly came on me that my despairing thoughts about my own small piece of work – the feeling that it makes no difference whether I do it or not – what's the use? – that there is the canker in my life, and not to finish the work I have begun is a sin. It's what the Desert Fathers called *accidie*, a kind of melancholy that paralysed the soul. 'Whatever thy hand findeth to do, do it with all thy might.' It is partly humility, partly fatigue, but I've got to get out of it, and already I have begun to feel a kind of rustling among the leaves.

In spite of Helen's long ties of affectionate friendship with Mary Ogilvie and her husband, Sir Frederick (at this period Director-General of the B.B.C.), her relationship with the Corporation was never a tranquil one, and soon after her return from Broadstairs she grumbles to Meg:

> Just at this moment I am dead stupid, for that idiotic B.B.C. suddenly wrote that they were doing *Time for Verse* on my Latin Lyrics, using such and such, introduction by . . . fees and so on, date Sunday, 6th June. I reared on my hind legs and said: 'Not 'arf you do, until I've seen the script.' The script arrives. Most of the linking bits were from my own work, but the Introduc-

tion – flowery and pretentious, full of mis-statements. . . . 'With the accession of Theodoric the Goth the light of Roman culture died in Europe'. To which I briefly replied that Theodoric the Goth had a passion for Latin culture and the fine arts, restored the walls of Rome, encouraged learning and music: in short was a more civilised human being than most of the Roman emperors who preceded him. (That he ended by killing Boethius was a pity, but they had been friends for years. Just that he had grown old and suspicious, and there *was* a conspiracy against him, and he thought Boethius knew. It was a political murder, first and last.)

That was a specimen, and the rest of it in language so rotund, such schoolgirl gush, that my spirit quailed. So I fell to and did something, and O.K. took it in this morning.

After the actual broadcast she has one brief comment for Meg: 'Val Gielgud said he had been in love with my Chinese lyrics all his life, and O.K. says the telephone in the Trade Dept. went all Monday asking for copies of my Latin ones.'

Helen reached her sixtieth birthday in May 1949, but her literary efforts seem mainly to have been in writing obituaries for old friends at their relations' request, or, as in Lord Londonderry's case, attending memorial services, neither activity being conducive to restoring or balancing her outlook on her own life.

To Meg:

One beautiful thing I saw was the memorial service for dear Londonderry in Westminster – with a great shaft of sunlight across the high arches of the transept. I didn't realise how fond I was of him till he was gone. It was a little like Basil Blackett; he had an extraordinary feeling for me – it came out in some of his letters – not amorous. One, I remember, said there were two people with whom he lived in a different world – one was Stanley Baldwin and one was me. And at the same time he could play the other game 'high and disposedly' as Queen

Elizabeth danced; and one misses the experts at that ancient pastime.

The notices about him in *The Times* were really charming – old Winterton remembering when he was 'Charlie', and the Air Force chiefs writing how he had fought for them when everybody was against them. And they all said, which I think was true, that he never said a hard word to anybody. Do you remember how kind he was when Jack tried to get Air Training at Oxford? And Jack's mischievous delight when he reported to me afterwards what Londonderry had said: 'You know, of course, that your aunt is the most charming woman in London?'

Then in December 1949 Helen's brother-in-law, Meg's husband, died. This was not unexpected; he was very old and had always had a weak chest. Helen had recently been at Kilmacrew and she wrote to Meg:

. . . My darling, your dear dear letter in this morning. And I wish I could just have got into a plane and gone straight to you. Again and again reading our little book (*Daily Light*), I think of you, and turn again to that marvellous July 26th – the entry that so comforted me the night you were engaged. . . . My love, my love, the life is very far back in you, and is it any wonder after these long years of grief and strain and worry about Daddy all the winters. And now the emptiness. But, dearest, if ever love's cup was full, it was in these last days. I do not think I shall ever see anything so beautiful as you two together.

Indeed I'll be proud to do what I can for his memorial. I don't suppose you have any record of Daddy Lusk's? It's only that so much of what I said about him would also apply to Daddy, and I wouldn't like to repeat any phrase. I am haunted by 'a lover of the countryside and his own people'.

A little later Helen says: 'I am so thankful that you liked what I wrote about Daddy. I am glad it contented his old friends.'

In 1950 Stephen Gwynn, an Irish poet and family friend, died:

Darling, this in haste. I wanted you and Mollie to get it quickly, for Stephen Gwynn did love you both.

The Times and *The Manchester Guardian* did him really well on Monday last, but *Time and Tide* and the *Spectator* so niggling and perfunctory that I just sat down and spent Friday and Saturday on this. I don't know what put Alcuin into my head, except that I was thinking of

> 'Few roads and far to gray Glencar,
> And life a-coasting fast,
> But there, mov'ron, should be thy throne,
> Could I win home at last.'

Stephen told me he had written it on his bicycle, a long long ride, with Elizabeth to see at the end of it, and in Glencar.

And I remembered Alcuin, very old, in Tours, far from the sea, and writing to a friend in England: 'Beside the shores of the white-winged sea, I wait the coming of the silent dawn, and I remembered that his fatherland was above Spurn Head: and the many things the two had in common rushed over me – and I got to work. And in some queer way this sort of filial pity has its reward, for I suddenly knew that I would write again, and working on the Alcuin material was like drinking at a spring well. I think he will be my last book – but I have a lot of poems for this one. I first read 'Few roads and far' when I was sixteen.

There are two letters to Siegfried Sassoon at this period:

Siegfried my very dear. This is only to say that I have been like a lost sheep for months, but the letters I *didn't* write were to the people I care for most. Then, mercifully, I got a touch of near-pneumonia and my sister came over to look after me. . . . And now they say I have got anaemia, but it's getting better, and I am delighted about it, because it explains my dreadful forgetfulness which was beginning to frighten me.

My love always

HELEN

The second letter is dated January 1950:

Dear Siegfried,

I think about you, and O.K. and I talk together about you with such deep affection and yet I never write. I have been making rather heavy weather this last year, fatigue, and the strange undying summer that was too uncanny to be gay. And a holiday postponed till November, too late for anything but gathering windfalls in the Kilmacrew orchards in the rain. And a kind of 'wan hope' (whatever that may mean). But now I am seriously assembling the scattered lyrics that I translated during the years at the office. And I begin to believe I'll some day write again (in spite of being poisoned last week with escaping ammonia, finally traced to a gash in the refrigerator); and also waking to find a torch ray crawling across the carpet at 4 a.m. But it wasn't a burglar – only a policeman pursuing an assumed burglar, having found our hall door wide to the wall. But it fair gave me a turn.

Bless you. Come back again and talk.

HELEN

In 1951 James Bridie, the Scottish physician and playwright died and Helen writes:

The other thing that shook me up was the news about James Bridie. O.K. is in real grief. And I keep remembering such endless jest and kindness for we were very fond of each other, and I did delight in him. And only 63 with all that harvest of wit and humanity still to be gathered in, and that gnome-like countenance twinkling at one. O.K. was reminding me that I was the first person to read his plays when the first batch came to Constable's – rather shaggy and untidy. And I read them and wrote: 'I think he is the successor to Shaw.'

Helen struggled on in a state of nervous tension, revealed assertively in letters to Meg, and more gently to Siegfried Sassoon. In the summer of 1950 she tells her sister:

I am almost addled with one of the jobs I most hate. The

Reprint Society are doing a special edition of *Peter Abelard* in their World Review Series. . . . O.K. thinks it is a good thing, but I doubt. However they wanted the usual autobiographical note 'As personal as possible', damn them. I said they could find it all in *Who's Who*, but they kept on at Constable's, and finally Ralph Arnold begged me to do something. It blocked every other thing in my head for days and days, and finally I did something that seemed to me execrable, but O.K. and Rosamond went off the deep end about it. One thing – the father of us both comes pretty well out of it, 'the Vicar of Wakefield turned Chinese scholar'. Tell me if you can bear it. It really made me a miserable witless animal for days. I think publicity makes me sicker even than it used to. And like you, I think public performances of any kind are major operations, and should not be enforced on the elderly.

Helen was not well enough to undertake the journey to Kilmacrew in the winter of 1952 for the wedding of Meg's eldest son, Sydney, to his brother George's widow, Ethel. It was a very happy occasion for all concerned and Helen's disappointment was acute. She ends a sad letter with a postscript:

Oh darling, don't say anything about it, but I somehow think O.K. feels he will soon have to slow down, and just go to the office now and then. We had a long talk together after breakfast, and I kept a solid countenance, but – the sword goes through one's heart. I don't think any of the others have suggested resignation to him, but I've noticed his weariness for a long time. It was one of the things that made it just impossible for me to get to the wedding. (I think I'll never got over it quite, for I felt so forlorn.) Don't worry about this, darling, it's only that you and I hate changes, and I can't bear O.K. feeling that he must give up any full connection with Constable's, but he'd still be on tap as adviser. And anyhow he's tired, tired.

O.K. did not resign from Constable's until the winter of 1953. He vacillated for a long time, even after the death of his faithful secretary, Mr Bates, who had worked for him for many years and taken over much responsibility from him. When the difficult decision had taken place his depression lifted and Helen wrote to Meg: 'O.K. is his old self again, happily planning a farewell party for everyone at the office, and deeply touched and pleased at the affection shown there to him.'

Helen attempted to write to her sister for another year or two, but her letters become confused scraps. There is, perhaps, one break in the silence. In 1955, when she and O.K. were at Kilmacrew, the Northern Ireland Station of the B.B.C. asked for an interview. O.K. persuaded Helen to read parts of an unused broadcast of hers on 'The Art of Translation', interspersed with personal comments. A pathetic scene ensued in the drawing-room of Kilmacrew House. A team came out from Belfast; the interviewer was tactful. Helen read her paper with Mollie sitting beside her to guide and encourage. The result was successfully adapted by the B.B.C., and they produced a recording which is still obtainable. It was hailed with optimistic relief and delight by all who heard it.

CHAPTER XXIII

Illness and Death

In the ensuing years the pace of Helen's illness increased, still gradually, but more and more definitely. Her local doctor sought advice from consultants and she underwent specialist treatment all without avail. The earlier intermittent bouts of loss of memory and oblivion of surroundings, settled finally into complete failure to recognise even the people she loved most – her nearest relatives, her dearest friends. There were no exceptions. She was unaware of O.K.'s death in 1958. She did not suffer, she was not unhappy. She smiled gently to herself and knew no one.

The Primrose Hill Road house was given up, and she was placed in the care of Mrs Luff, who had been her housekeeper and friend for many years. Her relations flew over from Kilmacrew, other friends visited her regularly, and of course her doctor. Flowers were delivered weekly under a standing order from Leonard Brockington, the well-known Canadian broadcaster.

In March 1965 pneumonia followed an attack of bronchitis. She died a few days later in a nursing home.

Helen was buried among her forbears in the graveyard of the ruined church of Magherally about two miles from Kilmacrew House. A winding path curves up the hill between the graves and the wind-swept trees. Here she sleeps in a spot of her heart's desiring with a view on all sides of the rolling hills, the green fields, the hedges and trees, with just an occasional glimpse of a cottage chimney or the whitewashed wall of a farmhouse. Indeed, Helen lies at peace in the land and among the people she loved and understood best.

The funeral service took place in the Magherally Presbyterian Church where her brother-in-law, the Rev John Dunwoodie

Martin, had been the minister for so many years before his death in 1949. Mollie Martin describes it as follows:

> The funeral was beautiful in its simplicity and just what Helen herself would have loved. From the plain white-washed church we climbed up the winding path with the sun shining and the snow still white at the backs of the ditches. And there, set in the hill is the shabby old graveyard; no paths, just worn tracks through the grass-grown graves and a distant background of the Mourne mountains. Mother and I went up the next day and the place was like a benediction. Mother is very, very tired, but in a strange way the last troubled years have fallen away, and the old Helen has returned – 'I had lost Helen and she has come back to me' – and she is comforted. I am sending Dr. Anderson's address. He is at least half a saint and wholly a scholar.

This is a quotation from Dr Anderson's address:

> No wonder *The Times* in its obituary wrote: 'Helen Waddell stood out for the grace of her learning, her love of fine literature and her poet's gift of translation. Others have conveyed, in sympathetic commentary and in accomplished English versions, the felicity of the secular Latin lyrics of the ninth to the twelfth centuries, but few have interpreted so well its poetic impulse, or captured with so haunting an effect the tenderness and passion to which it rises'.

Two letters of condolence, both sent to Meg, stand for the tribute of a very large number of relatives and friends who knew, appreciated and loved Helen in her lifetime. The first is from her nephew, Dr Mayne Waddell of Glossop:

March 1965

My dear Meg and Mollie,

Thank you for phoning me to give me the sad news about Helen. Just what can one say?

That happy adorable creature, the very essence of human kindness and compassion, loving all and loved by all: whose scholarly brilliance far from setting her in the clouds above us all seemed to enrich her understanding of simple things and simple people; who might so easily have sought after self and, by so doing, have achieved the highest honours that man could bestow upon her. And yet, with utter selflessness, she chose instead to occupy that wonderful brain with the day-to-day problems of the large brood of family chickens which she had gathered under her wings. For indeed that is how I picture her so often – as a kind of all-embracing foster-mother to the Waddells and their marital offshoots. And now we have her no more.

My own immediate reaction is not of sadness and sorrow, but of anger – an intense blazing anger at *war* and its futility. Here was this lovely genius, just about to blossom into the full bloom of her brilliance, when the war came along and diverted the floodwaters of her scholarly greatness into some stagnant backwater, wherein the daily chore of others' humdrum routine work left no time for the fruition of her own talents. It is maddening to think of it.

And yet so noble was her nature, so great the strength of character that she never showed by word or deed the utter frustration that must have been consuming her inside. There was no bitterness. Majestically she rose above all her disappointments and became once again the foster-mother to whom her war-weary chicks limped back. They didn't all return, but I am quite sure that, in Helen's mind, the missing chicks were somehow still under her wings.

The rest is sadness – I just think all the strain over the years had been too great.

And yet it is not all on the debit side. We have been fortunate to have known, to have loved and been loved by, perhaps, the greatest woman-scholar of our age. We have been fortunate to have had from time to time the benefit of her advice and good sense. But perhaps, above all we have been privileged to have witnessed the Christlike example of humility and utter selflessness which Helen so unwittingly gave us.

My love to you both,

MAYNE

The second comes from Gladys Bendit, better known as 'John Presland', who lived close to Helen in her years at Primrose Hill Road.

6th March, 1965

Helen Alford rang me yesterday evening and told me that Helen died early yesterday morning.

You must not grieve, you must try to be glad that the long eclipse is over and that in a sense Helen is returned to you as you always knew and loved her. For me, when I saw her picture in *The Times* obituary all the wonderful memories of the many years I knew and loved her came flooding back, obliterating the last sad recollections. I thought of the first time I met her at Basil Blackett's, small, slight, vital, crowned with what I always called her 'silver helmet' of hair. I remembered our many hours together, our talks which ranged from Alcuin to our party frocks! For I think I knew Helen from the everyday to the heights of inspiration. I remembered the music of her voice reading to me, and the flashes of her whimsical humour that would flash out unexpectedly. And behind all the charm and intelligence the noble generosity of her soul. That has come back and we must rejoice.

Ralph Arnold summed up Helen's life in one sentence: 'It is a transient tragedy (more tragic than most transient lives) redeemed, justified and lightened by an enduring monument of prose and verse.'

After Helen's death, and after giving Monica Blackett carte blanche to quote 'whatever you need' from his letters, Siegfried Sassoon wrote:

As for all who loved Helen and admired her, the eclipse of her magnificent intelligence was a disaster to me. I had come to feel that she was one of the people on whom I most depended for spiritual sustainment.

I have often wondered whether that healing beneficence which she gave to us contributed to her decline. She was spending herself all the time, wasn't she? And – who knows – her great spirit may be with me while I write these words. For such is my belief, thank God.

As you say, you have an immensely difficult task to complete, for, among all the modern writers, Helen possessed a unique quality of integrity and illuminativeness. It shines in all her perfected work, and is there in those letters of hers which I have seen.

And Lord David Cecil wrote:

I only met Helen Waddell once, thought her absolutely delightful. And I have always been an enthusiastic admirer of her work. I am deeply honoured that she and you liked mine.

I remember so well meeting her by chance at Constable's, our publishers, and her glowing warm spontaneous personality – and that she said she liked my first book, recently out, *The Stricken Deer* – and how I glowed and flushed, blushed with pleasure in response.

Helen herself told me that her biography was in her writings, poetry and prose alike, and that her sole aim had always been for her work to be 'great' – and consistently 'great'.

The standard she set herself could only be achieved at a price her body was not prepared to pay – in frustration, in nervous tension, in acceptance of other people's demands, in overwhelming circumstances, notably during the Second World War. She, with her courageous receptivity, her profoundly wise insight, and perhaps, most of all her belief in utter self-renunciation as the gateway to life and light, was bound inevitably to be broken by the conflict of body and spirit.

Her spirit passed on first to the 'excess of light' which she once translated as 'Thou art the journey and the journey's end'. When her body died she gained 'the freedom of heaven' at last, and for ever.

Appendix I

MEDIEVAL SOJOURN

It was, I think, in the spring of 1913 that I first made up my mind some day to write a book on Abelard and Héloise: so that *Peter Abelard*, published in England in May of 1933, had been at the back of my imagination for twenty years. I knew nothing then beyond the *Letters*, written long after the calamity that drove Abelard to the cloister, and Héloise to take the veil at Argenteuil: and I was bewildered, as I think most readers are, by the contrast in the two natures, the absolute passion of hers, the chill restraint of his: for I was too young and too crude to realise, as AE did when he first read them, that 'by being cold and pedantic he was trying to save her soul, and there was as much love in his reticence as in her outpouring.' For years after that my work lay in the Middle Ages, at first in medieval France, but finally in medieval humanism and poetry: and the first result of it was published in *The Wandering Scholars* and in *Medieval Latin Lyrics*. Here again I was baffled by the enigma of this man who was a famous poet of France, yet only his religious verse remains: whose thought was a wind and a fire that kindled the young men of Europe, and whose surviving prose is cold, austere and grey: who was twice condemned as a heretic, and died 'Christ's philosopher': and like Peter the Venerable, abbot of Cluny, who absolved him on his deathbed, I marvelled at the man who had once had the proudest name in France, now 'humbler than St Martin, lowlier than St Germain.' The tragedy of his life too perplexed me: for here was a man who followed after truth and served, as one of his contemporaries said, the soul of understanding in things, broken by hammerstroke after hammerstroke of the judgment of God. It was a long time before I saw that the reconciliation of his tragedy is the reconciliation of *Lear*: the breaking and transfiguring of a great egotism into something like sainthood: as though Lucifer should die a St John.

Even after I had seen this, I was in doubt as to whether the book should be a biography or a novel. I was in Paris at this time, staying in the American University Club in the old Hotel de Chevreuse: and my room had a balcony that looked out on the cobblestones of the Rue de la Grande Chaumière. There was a little *location* for handcarts in it, I remember, and they trundled over the cobblestones every morning at four, and wakened me irretrievably for the day. But in June of 1924, Paris took me literally by the throat: and I finally found myself being nursed by the nuns of the order of St Joseph in a room in the Institut Pasteur: one of them was a Breton, one a compatriot of mine, from Tory Island off the coast of Donegal, who had been in the Place de la Concorde twice in twenty-seven years. My throat was painful, and for four days and nights I could not sleep: the most profitable four days and nights I ever spent, for on the fourth night, after Sœur Louise had left me, I passed, fully awake and not I think delirious, into some strange state of being. For suddenly I was Héloise, not as I had ever imagined her, but an old woman, abbess of the Paraclete, with Abelard twenty years dead: and I was sitting in a great chair lecturing to my nuns on his *Introductio ad Theologiam*. It was near the end of the lecture, and I pronounced the benediction, and sat watching them go out, two by two. And one of them, the youngest and prettiest of my nuns for whom I felt some indulgence, glanced at me sideways as she went out, and I heard her whisper to the older sister beside her, '*Elle parle toujours Abelard*.'

It stabbed me. And even when the first hurt of it was past, the realisation that what was once a glory in men's minds had become an old woman's wearisome iteration, I began wondering if it were indeed true: if after all these years I were lecturing on this theology for the sake of now and then naming his name. And from that I began to remember that his theology had been condemned as heresy: and – for by this time Abelard had done his work upon me and had brought me to some sense of God – I began to wonder if I had perilled the souls in my charge by teaching them heretical doctrine for the sake of gratifying this ancient lust. And from that there stirred in me again the old dread for Abelard's own soul. But I remembered that Peter the Venerable had absolved him on his deathbed and had sent me the copy of the absolution, signed with his seal: and I rose and went to the ark where the charters of the convent were kept, and took from it the parchment of the absolution: and I sat there hour after hour, fingering the rough edges of the great seal of Cluny in my hands, and finding some dim comfort in it. Then the morning came, and with no sense of transition I was myself, but with full awareness of the other who I had been all the night before: and when the Mother Superior came to see me during the morning, I laughed and said, '*Ma Mère*, I too was an Abbess all last night.'

I told this to AE, because after he had read *Peter Abelard* he wrote to me that he could see I had lived into it as if I were a contemporary, 'as indeed you may have been in some deep of your being. There is an Everliving in which past, present and future are one, and when we brood on the past it may be our intensity brings us to live in that we brooded upon. It is not only in vision we revisit the past: our hearts may sink into it and know what others have known. This is a kind of faith with me.'

I do not myself know what the truth of the experience may have been: but after it I knew that I would certainly write about Abelard, and that the book would be a novel. I dared not read George Moore's *Héloise and Abelard* lest that wizard prose of his should come between me and these two so sharply remembered in my own mind, and even now I have not read it, because I have still to write the second part of the story as Héloise saw it, who survived him so many years: this second part is to be called *Héloise*. I do not know when it will be written. *Peter Abelard* took seven years.

Appendix II

POETRY IN THE DARK AGES

The Eighth W. P. Ker Memorial Lecture given on October 28th 1947

The memory of Scotland is long; she does not easily forget her dead. Of all the old Feasts, this that is due two nights from now, Hallowe'en, Vigil of All Saints and of All Souls, is more honoured here than in any of these islands. And though it is pleasant to reflect how ferociously W. P. Ker would have rejected ascription of sanctity, an older medievalist, John of Salisbury, secretary to Thomas Becket, declared that the saint is the man in bonds to truth: and in that bondage, the humanist who died on a mountain top at the age of 68, joyously and vigorously pursuing the freedom of his own will, was content to serve.

It is, I fear, a kind of effrontery to offer as his memorial lecture a subject in which the master of us all so proved his mastery. Yet it was, if you will believe me, not so much presumption as gratitude, a kind of *pietas*. It was W. P. Ker's *The Dark Ages*, a small book but with the quality of radium, that brought me, more than a quarter of a century ago, to Boethius, 'with whom is no small part of our eternity.' The *Consolation of Philosophy* had power upon me even then: I think there is indeed no generation that has not listened to it, hearing in it a kind of Angelus, rung in the evening of the ancient world. But these were the early twenties of this century; the good years when the Peace was not yet half a decade old and Locarno hung over Europe like a harvest moon, not yet a paper lantern with its sides stove in: one read it with a kind of detached romantic sensibility, very much as one construed at sixteen the autumnal prose of Cicero, conversing of Friendship and Old Age and Death: read it as Boethius himself admits he used to read philosophy, secure in his library with its walls of ivory and crystal. But when the veiled figure stands beside him in Theodoric's dungeon at Calvenzano, ante-chamber to torture and death, and looks upon him with more than mortal eyes, the moment of recognition is not for him only. That moment came, for Europe, in September of 1938. 'Consider,' wrote John of Salisbury, 'the image of that time when all the affairs of the subject are disposed at one strong man's nod: and those subjects prepared, albeit with sinking heart, to pronounce sentence of exile or death upon themselves. . . . *Hinc inde potestas terribilis* – hence a terrible power. To this pitch indeed, that the priests dissemble the commands of the Divine Law, that men are old without wisdom, that a judge sits ignorant of law, a prelate knows nothing of authority nor his people of discipline, that a man free born shall spurn his liberty, and a whole nation its quiet and its peace.' It is too savage a denunciation to fasten on the great Theodoric, who only in old age came to the corruption of absolute power: but in defiance of that corruption his friend Boethius died, in torture and in magnanimity.

Here, if the road shall bring thee back,
   The road thou hast forgot yet still dost seek,
'Look', thou wilt say, 'I do remember it,
Here was I born, and here I stay my feet:
   This is my fatherland.'
And if thou hast a mind to turn thy head
   And look again
Upon the night that thou hast left behind
   Lying upon all lands,
Then shalt thou see
The tyrants whom their wretched people dread
   Themselves are exiled men.

I have yet another apology to make: even the title of this lecture is not accurate. I have offered you *Poetry in the Dark Ages*, and it should have been *Latin Poetry in the Dark Ages*. There was poetry, and great poetry, in the countries that lay outside the ever-narrowing shadow of Rome: the northern tongues, Old High German, Old English, Icelandic, these had their rich harvest in epic, as Ireland in lyric: but in these languages I have no skill, and no right to speak. For them, the Dark Ages were high noon: but in the Latin countries, Italy and France and Spain and Roman Africa,

> '. . . thou see'st the twilight of such day
> As after sunset fadeth in the west;'

'mere glimmerings and decays.' It is true that by the eleventh century the tide is coming in again, in Latin, and above all in the younger languages that drew from the Latin deep: Provençal lyric, the *chanson de geste*, the new poetry in Northern Italy, and soon to come the 'living and victorious splendours' of the Latin hymns of the twelfth century and the twinkling tavern lights of the Goliard verse. But it is the forgotten generations, the obscure poets of an obscure age, that are the business of this lecture: the men who taught Latin grammar and wrote their clumsy verse and copied the manuscripts of greater poets than themselves, through the centuries of the barbarian invasions, the savage tides that swung back and forth through the breached walls of Rome and Ravenna and Trèves and Padua and Aquileia and Arles: poets indifferent in scholarship and halting in metre, but they kept the tradition of civilisation alive, and they were good company in the darkness that came at one stride over Europe, in the autumn of 1939. They might be, as Goldsmith who loved them saw them, 'busy with a petty traffic in a little creek': but they were dredgers that kept the channels open to the trade routes of the ancient world, to the pagan authors with whom, said Milton, 'is bound up the life of human learning'.

Now these are swelling claims, and the language, I fear, a little swollen. Can it at all be justified?

> Man's life, it knows not what shall be
> Of slaughter or security,
> If Death shall come
> With Hesperus or with the morning star.
> The darkness holds us down,
> Fate is unknown,
> And Time so brittle in the times that are.

That is Venantius Fortunatus, come from Trieste to sixth-century France, and sickened at the brutalities that lay behind the lavish hospitality of the Merovingian kings.

By these, by these same chains, O Rome,
   Thou art more strong,
   Thy faith more absolute
   Against the wrong.
For ever art thou free: what bonds avail
When he hath touched them who absolveth all?
That heart unconquered and these solemn walls
Shall stand, shaken it may be, not destroyed
By any trampling of the hosts of hate.
That road is closed to war, whose gate
Stands open to the stars.

That is Arator, sixth century, reading to the Roman crowd in the church of St Peter ad Vincula, St Peter in chains, with the Goths hovering for the kill: revised by Alcuin, two centuries later. A century earlier, the hawk was Attila, and one may see in Raphael's cartoon the sky-towering presences of St Peter and St Paul defending the city of their martyrdom against that figure of nightmare. But there was another city, only less proud than Rome, and no saint defended her. Attila had his will of her, and long after, Paulinus of Aquileia wrote of her in the greatest, perhaps the loveliest, lament of the Dark Ages.

Lament for Aquileia destroyed, and never to be built again

To weep thine ashes am I come,
   And have no tears.
All words are withered and the heart is numb
   With too much grief.

Time was that thou hadst all,
Beauty and wealth and state,
Gallant thy wall,
Gallant the citizens that made thee great.

Thy churches blazed with light,
  Strong was thy hierarchy:
Thou the cathedral city, thou didst hold
  Venetia's self in fee.

Puissant in all delights
  Thy pride swelled higher,
Provoked the eternal Judge,
  Challenged His ire.

The wrath of God went forth,
  Stirred up a cruel race,
Hastened them riding from the rising sun
  To work thy doom.

Came godless Attila,
  Fierce, cruel, merciless,
Swept round thee his great wheel,
  Five hundred thousand men.

He saw the storks that nested in thy towers
Come flying through the fields, carrying their young.
  He knew it for a sign: he knew
  Thine hour was come.

He bade his army strike,
  The walls are battered down,
The city's fallen, burning,
  Beat level with the ground.

  Was ever day like this?
Here raged the fire, and yonder raged the sword.
  They had no mercy on the women there,
  Nor on the young.

They dragged them captive, whom the sword had left,
  Young men and old, women and little lads,

That which had scaped the fire the plunderers
    Took for their own.

The books of Holy Writ,
All that the scholars' genius had revealed,
Went to the bonfire, burnt to satisfy
    Their ignorant heathen hate.

Dead lie the priests of God;
No man to give their bodies burial.
Hands bound behind their backs, the living go
    Captive to slavery.

The sacramental cup in hands most foul,
Whatever faithful souls had given to God,
Cast lots for, carried off to foreign lands,
    To come again no more.

O thou that once didst hold thy head so high,
    How low thou liest, and how useless now;
Crushed beneath thine own ruins, never more
    In any age to be rebuilt again!

No sound of singing now,
    Silent organ and lute.
There is a sound of sorrow and of crying,
    No sound of children playing in the house.

City of nobles, now the peasants crouch
    In cellars underground,
City of princes, thy best shelter now
    A poor man's hut.

Streets of great houses rearing up to heaven,
    Snowy with marble curiously wrought,
Harvest of hay now, that the country folk
    Bind with a scanty rope.

The churches of the Saints, with princes thronged,
Are thick with briars now,
Alas, they are become a shelter now
For fox and snake.

Throughout all countries art thou bought and sold.
No rest is in thee even for the dead.
Their bodies are flung out from the very tomb
– The market's brisk for marble.

Yet vengeance hath o'ertaken with thyself,
Him that destroyed thee:
The fires of Hell, the gnawing worms
Are fast on Attila.

O Christ our King, the Judge no man gainsays,
Look down in pity, turn away Thy wrath.
Forbid a fate the like of this to fall
Again upon Thy folk.

We bring Thee hymns and prayers,
Rein in the peoples, curb the envious,
Protect us ever with Thy strong right arm,
Thou that hast mercy on men everywhere.

Chasten us, Father, but be merciful.
Go Thou before Thy flock, and come behind:
Thy folk that walk upon a harmless road
Keep Thou for ever more.

Small and clear as in a crystal, one sees in it the many towns so beautiful, and they all dead do lie. But there is hope of a tree if it be cut down that it will sprout again and the tender branch thereof will not cease. Aquileia is still a silent place, a cathedral of the eleventh century brooding over a sickly hamlet and a desolate plain: but the remnants of her folk, with the poor tributaries of the sister towns that Attila destroyed, made their way to the no man's land between the waters, that now is Venice: and by the tenth century Torcello raised its single campanile above the lagoons and the white thorn blossom, and inlaid its incomparable mosaic to take away the reproach of a century barren of beauty. And this is why the literature of these centuries is good reading for contemporary Europe. She had come through so much: she will come through this thing also. These men, like ourselves, had lived in a trance-charmèd world, the Pax Romana, like the Pax Britannica, brooding over

> The blue Mediterranean where he lay
> Lulled by the coil of his crystalline streams.

Rome, to them, was a thing that could not be shaken. Even so fierce an antagonist of paganism as Tertullian called Rome 'sacrosanct': without her could be no stability. To Lactantius, who had suffered in the persecutions of Diocletian, she was, under God, the one bulwark of society: beyond her was Chaos and old Night. Alaric the Goth essayed twice to attack her, and twice, as in some superstitious awe, withdrew. It was unthinkable that she go down. Even when in the first years of the fifth century she had to call home the legions to defend her, Claudian could see cause only for pride, not foreboding. The lines describing that recall are among his loveliest: and he knew nothing of their tragic irony.

> 'Even as the cattle in the winter woods,
> Hearing their master's old familiar shout,
> Come shouldering down to the remembered pastures
> Deep in the valley, answering faithful lowing,
> And through the twilight of the naked branches
> Glints the last straggler's horn:
> So came the legions from the uttermost isles
> Of Britain, where they held the Scots in leash,
> And those that were a wall against the Ruhr,
> And cowed the churls of Hesse and Thüringen,
> They've turned the splendid menace of their line

Against the threat to Italy: they're gone.
The right bank's naked of its garrison.
Naught but the terror of the Roman name
Defends an open frontier.
To-night there is no watch upon the Rhine.'

Within about a twelvemonth the barbarians had swept across France: they were in the vineyards of Bordeaux: they were encamped beneath the Pyrenees. All France, said St Orientius, 'smoked like a funeral pyre'. This was in 406: four years later, Alaric was in Rome, and she was taken that had taken all the world.

Yet it was Alaric, not Rome, that died. And when her hour came, although she died, she died in childbirth, and the child that was born of her was Europe.

It was indeed expedient that Rome should die, the Rome of intolerable contrasts and crazy economy: a half-Oriental and evil Court (though I confess I have a heart for that Emperor who kept hens – most of them had less respectable pets): at the bottom, a slave population that bred like maggots and stank to heaven: a class above them that brawled and bawled and squandered and was given free bread and races (chariot, not dog) to keep them quiet: above them, a harried middle-class of unpaid civil servants to struggle with administration and the fantastic finance of the Empire. That Rome was better dead: and one man saw it, as early as the first century.

The Roman was the victor of the world.
All seas, all lands, the journeys of the sun,
Aye, and the moon,
He owned them all and was not satisfied.
The fretted seas he sent this way and that
With his great-bellied keels: if round yon headland
A little bay lay hid, or distant land
That cropped with gold, she was the enemy;

The obedient oracles for war stood ready,
The hunt for wealth was up.
He had no pleasure in familiar things
That please the common folk: the well-worn joys
That poor men's hands have handled. Out at sea
Soldiers would prate about the bronze of Corinth;
The purple that was once got from the shellfish
Is dull stuff now, beside their chemicals.
The men of Africa have cause to curse them.
China's despoiled of silk, Arabia
Hath stripped her incense-fields.
Always fresh killing and new wounds of peace . . .
They hew the citron tree in Africa . . .
And make their tables of its gold-flecked surface,
And round that barren and ignoble wood
Gather a crowd of men sodden with drink,
And yon mercenary swills the wealth of the world.
Rust on his idle sword. . . .

The self same madness is in politics:
Easy to buy a Roman citizen:
He'll sell you his vote any day for a bucket-shop share
Or a spot of cash. The man in the street's for sale,
And so is the man in the House: they all have their price.
The pristine liberal virtue of the old men
Has dropt away, the power they had they lost
Scrambling for gold, their ancient dignity
Rotted by money, trodden under foot.
They set the mob on Cato, drove him out,
And now they are more sick at heart than he.
The man's abashed that took his office from him.
Here is the symbol of a people's shame,
The ruin of their standards:
When they beat the old man up, sent him to exile,
It was no man they banished,
It was the honour and the power of Rome.

Lost, lost is Rome, her own self her own prey.
She hath made herself a spoil and there is none
That will avenge her.
This flooding sewer of money out at interest
Has caught the common folk in a double whirlpool.
Their usury has choked them.
Not a house but is mortgaged, not a man but in pawn.
Like a disease hatched in the silent cells
This madness rages through their harried bodies,
Baying them down.
Men ruined think of robbery in arms:
The good things luxury has spent and spoiled
They'll win again by wounds:
Your beggar dare be bold: he has naught to lose.
There's Rome asleep in the gutter, snoring fast.
And what's to wake her?
Sound reason or the arts?
Or naught but war and madness and the lust
That's wakened by the sword?

Now, the man who wrote that was no ascetic of the new faith, no wild-eyed hermit from the Desert. He was Petronius, Arbiter of Elegance at Nero's court, an aristocrat who had been an admirable provincial governor in the old tradition, and then came back to Rome, drifting like some ironic figure of the nineties into that insane world, recording, one may imagine, night after night in the *Satiricon*, as it might be in *Ulysses*, the civilisation that he relished, and sickened at. He died by his own hand in the sixties of the first century. In A.D. 68 Nero too was dead, in the thirty-first year of his age.

I have said that it was expedient Rome should die. For one must die to become a legend: and the Roman legend was the creative inspiration of Europe. Her decadence was forgotten: what lived was her language, her literature, her law, the roads that were as forthright as her justice, and, despite some remembered cruelty – her magnanimity. Claudian had written of her, not of her armed might, but of her gentleness.

'For it was she alone who took
Her vanquished to her breast,
And cherished all mankind, naming one name,
In fashion of a mother, not a mistress.
She conquered men, and called them citizens,
And those that were afar off she brought nigh.'

A few years after that first sack by Alaric the Goth in 410, Rutilius Namatianus could cry to her from far at sea, as if the garland of her war had never withered.

'Thou hast made one fatherland out of many nations.
Thou hast made thy prisoners thy friends.
Thy conquered are thy comrades in the war,
Thou hast made a city of that which was a world.'

It is a strange thing to remember, thinking of the centuries of her dying – for she was a great while dying: one loses count of her sieges and her conquerors – that in the meridian of her power, the noontide peace of the Augustan summer, she herself looked back to her beginnings in a conquered city and a burning town: and the man who gave her immortality was the hollow-cheeked sad-eyed Virgil of the Hadrumetum mosaic. The Aeneid is not a popular schoolbook, nor the hero of it always a heroic figure: but if all else goes from the schools, let us at least keep the second book of Virgil. I speak of it with passion, for after half a lifetime of neglect, something sent me to it on that September afternoon when the Luftwaffe first broke through the defences of London, and that night it seemed as though London and her river alike burned. You remember the cry of Aeneas waking in the night, *O lux Dardaniae!* (the cry that someone copied in a manuscript of the eleventh century in Canterbury), the rush, arming as he went, into the street, his halt with the distraught old priest carrying his little grandson and his conquered gods, the hurried question – 'Where's the fighting now?' – and the answer –

'Come is the ending day, Troy's hour is come,
The ineluctable hour.
Once were we Trojan men,
And Troy was once, and once a mighty glory
Of the Trojan race.
But God in wrath has taken it all from us,
And given it to the Greeks.
Troy's burnt.
And now they lord it in the gutted town.'

You remember the wild confused street-fighting in the light of the fires and the half-light of the moon, the young men recognising him and shouting for his leadership –

'O boys, O strong of heart in vain,
If you've a mind to follow one who dares
The ultimate strait, look first and see the hand
That Fate hath dealt us.
The gods by whom our empire stood have left us,
Have quit their altars and their empty shrines.
You rush your succours to a gutted town.
Let's on to death, crash down amid their swords.
There's one security for conquered men,
And that's to hope for none.'

They follow him like men athirst for death – wolves under the black arch of the night: there is the growing desperation, the horror of Priam's end, the final decision, and the escape, star-guided, to the hills, with his old father on his back, his little son by the hand: the halt on the hill, the realisation that Creusa his wife is not behind him, the crazed search – how often have these last years seen the like of it – through burning streets and crashing walls, the heroic Godspeed from that wan courageous ghost, speaking from the other side of death, and his heartbroken return. He climbs the hill again: the verse drags and dulls: he finds them, the housefolk and a herd of fugitives, soldiers, mothers, and most piteous of all, *collectam exsilio pubem*, a huddle of young things gathered up for exile. I saw them, the young things gathered up for exile, with their little bags and bundles, at the end of that cloudless, endless September day, when the mother and babies were herded out of London: now at evening huddled like lambs in a green field after a whole day's travelling, and bleating like lambs 'with their weak human cry' – *collectam exsilio pubem*. And the night passes, and the morning star climbs above Mount Ida, and Aeneas looks down, and sees Troy burning still, and the Greeks at every gate.

'I gave it up. I took the old man on my back and made for the hills.'

There the book ends. That is how Virgil saw the beginning of Rome, *Roma immortalis*, golden Rome: a battered soldier, leading a handful of refugees. This is the pattern of history; and perhaps it is the pattern of eternity, translated into time.

'There, dying on the cross, the world's life hung,
Laving a world's sin in that deathly tide.
That downbent head raised earth above the stars.
O timeless wonder! Life, because one died.'

Now the sack of Troy is a far cry from the Dark Ages, but it is the key to them. That inheritance of glory and of tragedy was the patrimony of Rome. Hardly one of the barbarians who conquered her but claimed an ancestor who had fought on the losing side at Troy. These men had seen some majesty. Troy's successor, Rome, was Prospero to their Caliban, and on the whole they were good monsters. Apollinaris Sidonius, Roman patrician and Bishop in Auvergne, was head and front of the *Résistance* when the Burgundians came, was captured by them, held a year in prison, released, and adored by them to the day of his death. But in the interval, a friend writes asking him to compose an Epithalamium for a marriage feast. Here is his reply.

To Catulinus that he cannot write him an Epithalamium because of the enemy hosts

How should I, even if I could,
  Write you Epithalamium,
Set down among these hairy hordes
  And suffering their German?
I dine with them and with wry face
  Praise all they choose to utter,
They sing full-fed Burgundian songs,
  And oil their hair with butter.

Wouldst know what terrifies my Muse,
  What is it she complains on?
How can she write a six foot line
  With seven feet of patron?
O happy eyes! O happy ears!
  Too happy, happy nose,
That smells not onions all day long.
  For whom no garlic grows!

They do not come to you at dawn,
  Breathing out leeks and ardour,
Great friendly souls with appetites
  Much bigger than your larder.
Nor do these hearty friends of mine
  Declare they look on thee
As Uncle Joe or Uncle Sam –
  But ah! they do on me.

It is a cartoon, in little, of the power in barbarian Europe of a conquered Rome. What of the surviving Europe that was not barbarian? Security was gone: the world had had yet another lesson in the impermanence of greatness. *Manet Oceanus*: there remained the *Civitas Dei*, the city that hath foundations, whose builder and maker is God. And that city, so obstinate is the heart of man, still lay upon the Seven Hills. Already in the sixth century Gregory the Great was building 'without sound of axe or hammer, a stronger house than Caesar's'. Alcuin, at the end of the eighth, lamenting the sack of Lindisfarne by the Danes, calls to mind his own sorrow at the sight of Rome,

'Rome, the crown and the flower, Rome that was golden,
A heap of wild ruins now, thy beauty down-beaten with swords.
A huddle of shabby roofs men see thee now,
Silent, sunken, alone';

but by the next century, her name is sung along the pilgrim roads – '*O Roma nobilis, orbis et domina*'.

– O Rome that noble art, and the world's lady,
Red with the roses and blood of the martyrs.
White with the lilies and light of the virgins,
Hail to thee, hail to thee, through all the fates that be,
Blessing be on thee, for ever and ever!

It was, I think, Lord Bryce who described the Roman empire as the mightiest ghost that ever troubled the affairs of living men. But to the Dark Ages, Rome was not politics, she was poetry; and in what was left of the ancient learning, Virgil was to them, as he was centuries later to Dante, the grave and gentle guide through the kingdoms of the dead. Those ages had need of the Virgilian tenderness, the language of the heart. And though the Church, officially, might deprecate that dangerous ancient power, it was in the quiet houses of religion, century after century, that the manuscripts would be copied and borrowed and collated:

'The evening star looks down on the long fast
Of men still reading.
And breaks for quiet hearts the holy bread.'

Now, what profit had they of their Virgil? A young acquaintance of mine, moved to explore for himself the vast quarry of the

Poetae Latini Carolini Aevi, retired from it as from the shores of the Dead Sea: and it must be confessed that a great deal of it is sad stuff. There are long dull metrical lives of saints: long dull series of inscriptions for altars and monuments: eccentric acrostics, formal letters in verse of congratulation, of condolence, of courtesy. Too often one seems to be sorting outmoded junk in a lumber-room rather than digging for a forgotten civilisation in a grave-mound. And suddenly, yawning, sifting, turning pages, you come on the epitaph of one dead at Roncesvalles.

> 'Buried in this low grave his pale limbs lie
> Whose spirit climbs the starry steep of heaven.
> Born of a famous stock, of the blood of France,
> All gifts of gentleness and noble living
> Were his but yesterday.
>
> The down of manhood on his rosy cheek
> Scarce fledged: alas, so youth and beauty died . . .
> The day King Charlemagne spurned under foot
> The soil of Spain, that day he died to the world,
> And now, where'er he be, he lives to God . . .
>
> Go with him, now, O Vincent, mighty martyr,
> Plead for him, blessed one, with the Most High.
> Here in his grave-mound though his body lie,
> He climbs the shining road, stands in God's House.
> And all ye Christian folk that cross the threshold
> Of this holy place, plead for him with the Son
> Begotten of the Father's heart, and say
> 'God in Thy mercy' – say ye all together –
> 'Redeem Thy servant Eghard from his sins.'

You read with respect for the grace and competence of the verse a ninth-century requiem for the abbess of Gandesheim, learned and young: and suddenly a lark rises at your feet.

Thou hast come safe to port
I still at sea,
The light is on thy head,
Darkness in me.

Pluck thou in heaven's field
Violet and rose,
While I strew flowers that will thy vigil keep
Where thou dost sleep,
Love, in thy last repose.

You read solemn interchange of compliment and valediction between the great ecclesiastics, the V.I.P.'s of the eighth and ninth centuries: the Archbishop of Sens suggests a visit to his old friend Alcuin: Alcuin replies: and suddenly his world is ours, and a little uneasy about the rations.

'There's a sorry little scrub that is servant unto me,
And at the statutory hours he feeds me every day.
He's my seneschal and butler,
He's the cook and the hostler,
And the laundryman and kitchen man and bootboy too.
But if I send him out on an errand down the street,
I know not how it is – but he never will come back . . .
Every man jack I have goes the selfsame way.
It's hunger thins my household and scatters my poor men,
Like a rascal tax collector that can never fill his wame.
So let you stay at Sens, my good bishop, where you still
Can keep your men about you and can let them eat their fill:
And let no fond hopes delude you to the sweet fields of the Sauer;
Believe me, my lord bishop, you are better where you are.
For whatever drink is to be drunk or meat upon a bone,
Believe me, my lord bishop, we can finish it at home.
You've the Yonne and the Saône to fill you full of fish,
And the vineyards of Sens, and sometimes to your dish,
Comes a good horned wether to get your blessing on it.
And all your hungry household can be let loose upon it,

To carve it up and eat it up and then sing grace.
So be mindful of poor Alcuin, you sitting snug and warm
In your own chimney corner – and the Lord bless you, Sam!

You will read page after page of inscriptions for altars, epitaphs for tombs, in this church and that throughout Charlemagne's empire, competent lapidary verse: and suddenly it takes wing, and St Michael stands in his angelic strength as on the eastern cliff of Paradise.

O Michael, servant of the eternal King,
Standing upon the citadel of Heaven
Amid thy winged comrades, through the years
Of the abiding light, the kingdoms of white peace:
Protect this altar which we dedicate,
On earth, to thee.

Theodulf the Spaniard, judge under Charlemagne of the southern circuit, has a considerable territory of informed, intelligent correct Latin verse, dull as only the informed, intelligent and correct can be: your eye is caught by an unusual title: '*Wherefore did the scars of Christ's Passion remain in the body of his Resurrection?*' You expect a piece of ingenious legalistic argument: this is what you find.

When Christ came from the shadows by the stream
Of Phlegethon,
Scars were upon his feet, his hands, his side.
Not, as dulled souls might deem,
That He who had the power
Of healing all the wounds whereof men died
Could not have healed his own,
But that those scars had some divinity,
Carriage of mystery,
Life's source to bear the stigmata of Death.

By these same scars his men
Beheld the very body that they knew,
No transient breath,
No drift of bodiless air,
And held him in their hearts in fortress there.
They knew their Master risen, and unfurled
The hope of resurrection through the world.

By these same scars, in prayer for all mankind,
Before his Father's face.
He pleads our wounds within his mortal flesh,
And all the travail of his mortal days,
For ever interceding for His grace,
Remembering where forgetfulness were blind,
For ever pitiful, for ever kind,
Instant that Godhead should take thought for man,
Remembering the manhood of His Son,
His only Son, and the deep wounds he bore.

By these same scars his folk will not give o'er
Office of worship, while they see,
Passion, thy mystery:
In those dark wounds their weal,
In that descent to Hell their climb to the stars,
His death, their life,
Their wreath, his crown of thorns.

There is nothing worthy to stand beside it in Carolingian verse. It looks back to the *Vexilla regis prodeunt*, and the *Crux fidelis* of Venantius Fortunatus, the sound far above singing: and forward to the

Adoro te devote,
O latens Deitas

of St Thomas Aquinas.

But for our human griefs, for the last Virgilian tenderness, read

Alcuin writing to the friend of all his life, Arno of Salzburg, so many leagues away.

> No mountain and no forest, land nor sea,
> Shall block love's road, deny the way to thee . . .
> Yet why must love that's sweet
> So bitter tears beget,
> Honey and gall in one same goblet set?
> Even so, O world, the feet
> Of sorrow follow hard upon delight,
> Joy breaketh in a cry,
> And all sweet things are changed to bitterness.
> They will not stay for me: yea, all things haste to die.
>
> Wherefore, O world,
> So soon to die,
> From us depart,
> And thou, my heart,
> Make haste to fly
> Where is delight that fades not,
> The unchanging shore,
> The happy house where friend from friend divides not,
> And what he loves, he hath for ever more.
> Take me, beloved, in thy prayer with thee,
> Where shall be no estranging thee and me.

These are the halcyon days of the Dark Ages: and they were brief. Alcuin dies, and Charlemagne dies, and the sons of the men whom Alcuin taught go down at Fontenoy in the fratricidal feud between Charlemagne's grandsons, the undying quarrel for the Rhine.

> 'Yea, but whether they be men of Charles or men of Louis there,
> Now the fields are bleached to whiteness with the white bones of the slain,
> Even as they bleach in autumn with the coming of the gulls:'

The chivalry of France is butchered, and France herself left naked to the Northmen. But the Northmen in their turn come under the yoke of Christ and of the ancient learning, and meantime that learning is journeying east, and will find asylum at Fulda and Reichenau and Tegernsee and St Gall. By the end of the ninth century Rome is paying tribute to the Saracens, but there is an anonymous poet to upbraid her with a *saeva indignatio* worthy of Swift. By the middle of the tenth century the Huns are in St Gall and have burned the library, but not the books. They were not there to burn, for they have been hurried down the mountain passes to Reichenau by the lake: and the Huns go, and the books come back, though not without suspicion and murmurings on the part of the original librarian. Meantime in England, as in Ireland, the Danes have sacked the ancient religious houses, Clonfert and Clonmacnoise, Lindisfarne and Jarrow and Hexham, 'where men so valiant and so great lights of the church lie and take their rest.' Northumbrian poetry falls silent: but by the end of the ninth century, Alfred is translating Boethius in the green shade of Winchester. He will translate

O stelliferi Conditor orbis

and he will remember the blackened fields of Northumbria, and his own gaunt hunted years.

'O Maker of the starry world,
Who, resting on thy everlasting throne,
Turnst heaven like a spindle,
And hast the stars brought under law,
So that the moon, now shining at the full,
Straight in the pathway of her brother's flame,
Blots out the lesser stars:
Now with her crescent dim
Draws near the sun and loses all her light:
And Hesperus, in the first hour of eve,
Awakens the cold welling of the stars,
And then as Lucifer

Grows pallid in the rising of the sun.
It is Thy power tempers the changing year
So that the leaves the North Wind swept away
The West Wind brings again.
Arcturus watched the sowing of the seed
That Sirius parches in the standing grain.
Naught is there that escapes the ancient law,
Or leaves the work of its appointed ward.
Thou guidest all things to their certain goal,
All but the ways of men:
Keep them in check Thou wilt not.
O Ruler of the world, Thou hast spat them out.
Why should the noxious consequence of sin
Take hold upon the sinless?
The pervert sits enthroned,
And ruffians set their heel on the neck of saints.
The just man bears the guilt of the unjust.
No perjury,
No fraud tricked out with gaudy lies,
Can damage evil men:
And when they have a mind to use their power
They take delight in subjugating kings
That kept the world in awe.
O Thou, who e'er Thou art,
Thou who dost bind all things in covenant,
Now, now look down on these unhappy lands.
We are not the vilest part of Thy creation,
Great though it be – men tossed on bitter seas.
Rein in the surging of wild rushing waters,
And Thou that rulest heaven's immensity,
By that same covenant, steady the earth.

It is the eternal cry of the clay to the potter, 'Why hast Thou made me thus?' He will translate it, and after many days he will translate the answer, which is no answer in logic, but in excess of light.

'O Father, give the spirit power to climb
To the fountain of all light, and be purified.
Break though the mists of earth, the weight of the clod,
Shine forth in splendour, Thou that art calm weather,
And quiet resting place for faithful souls.
To see Thee is the end and the beginning,
Thou carriest us, and Thou dost go before,
Thou art the journey, and the journey's end.'

Index

In this index HW = Helen Waddell

Margaret Waddell